THE
CONCISE HISTORY
OF
MODERN IRELAND

THE
CONCISE HISTORY
OF
MODERN IRELAND

RICHARD KILLEEN

GILL & MACMILLAN

First published in United Kingdom and Ireland, 2006
by Gill & Macmillan Ltd., Hume Avenue, Park West, Dublin 12, Ireland
with associated companies throughout the world
www.gillmacmillan.ie

ISBN-13: 978 07171 4069 5
ISBN-10: 0 7171 4069 5

A CIP catalogue record for this book is available from the British Library.

Design, Cartography and Picture Research: Red Lion Publishing

Printed and bound by Butler and Tanner, Frome

Typeset in Sabon and Trajan

CONTENTS

INTRODUCTION
MODERN IRELAND

The Concise History of Modern Ireland is a synoptic work that assumes no previous knowledge on the part of the reader. If this is your first introduction to the subject, it attempts to provide a lucid overview of the principal themes of Irish history in the modern era.

First, define your terms. Concise is tricky, in that it is an in-between category. Short means pocket-sized and very brief indeed, leaving little room for anything more than bare narrative. Contexts and continuities are heavily discounted. A full-length monograph or study, on the other hand, has all the room it needs for the elaboration of these subtleties. The short account is designed for those who want only the most summary overview: it will not satisfy the reader who wants a little more depth in the treatment. The monograph, contrariwise, is directed first and foremost at the specialist. Inevitably, it entails degrees of detail that are off-putting for the general reader. A concise history attempts to steer a course between these extremes, providing a reasonable amount of context and interpretation without overwhelming those not previously familiar with the ins and outs of the subject.

I can only leave it to the reader to decide if the present work fulfils that ambition or falls between two stools, the occupational hazard of all solutions that entail the splitting of differences and the reconciliation of opposites.

The real problem lies in defining 'modern'. This is a word and a concept that has produced a small library of work from scholars. In a European context, it can legitimately be dated at various points since 1500. From this date onward, Europe's exponential advance, relative to China, India and the Muslim world – all of which had previously outstripped it in key areas of human achievement and civilisation – was unquestioned. China retreated into an introverted self-regarding stagnation, symbolised by the end of its voyages of discovery. In 1421, it had sent the largest fleet the world had seen to date – 500 enormous ships, vastly bigger than anything any European shipyard could even dream of – on a series of exploratory voyages to the ends of the earth. In two years, they discovered Australia and New Zealand; sailed round the Cape of Good Hope and Cape Horn; circumnavigated Greenland and discovered both

North and South America. All this nearly a century before the European voyages of discovery. China's subsequent long isolation, only now coming to an end, should not blind us to its pre-eminence among world civilisations for much of recorded history.

As with China, so with India and the Muslim world. Centuries of scientific and cultural advance slowed around 1500. India was enervated by successive invasions from the north, of which Tamerlane's was the most terrible. The brilliance of Muslim cultural achievement also declined from the sixteenth century on. This was not at all obvious to contemporary Europeans. Although in 1492 Spanish Christian armies had finally destroyed the Muslim kingdom of Granada – the last vestige of the successively brilliant civilisations of al-Andalus which had existed for 700 years – the Ottoman threat subsisted. At the other end of the Mediterranean, Muslim power had captured Constantinople in 1453 and the Ottomans were to remain a potent threat to the south-eastern flank of the Christian world for another two hundred years. Twice – in 1526 and 1683 – Ottoman armies came within a whisker of capturing Vienna. Only with the failure of the latter attempt did the long Ottoman decline finally set in.

So, while not at all clear to contemporaries, 1500 represents a decisive turning point in the position of Europe relative to the other major world civilisations. The voyages of discovery; the scientific revolution; spectacular advances in literature, music, philosophy and architecture; the development of ever more sophisticated banking and finance systems and the enabling of commerce: all these things and more are plainly visible in Europe in the centuries since 1500. Moreover, the relative richness of the European achievement in that time is undeniable.

None the less, historians are uneasy about lumping the past half millennium into a single category. Within that period, there has been one further division that has usually been thought to mark a wholesale break with the past. The joint effect of the industrial revolution and the political revolutions in France and America called into existence new modes of thought, new sets of expectations, new means of organising people en masse, new assumptions about individual and political rights and systems, enormously expanded productive capacity and a quite sensational increase in total material wealth. The twin revolutions ushered in the age of nationalism and democracy and the rise of the city.

This process dates from about 1780. In a sense, it is still incomplete. We are all heirs to the changes it set in motion. We take it for granted that we have a vote, that we are all equal before the law, that we can travel easily and comfortably, that clean water is readily available to all, that sewerage systems will carry off our effluent without fuss, that we can be clean and not stink, that we will be more likely to live in a town than in the country, that our children will get an education and be literate and numerate, that we won't die prematurely of preventable diseases. None of these things could be taken for granted by Europeans before 1780.

And that is why historians distinguish between the Early Modern and the Modern. The former period covers the astonishing advances in Europe from 1500 to about 1780, symbolised by the achievements of Newton, Michelangelo, Descartes, Bach and a host of others. The period since 1780 is what is usually meant by 'modern' because of the wholesale revolution in productive capacity and mental assumptions that date from that time.

That is the definition of modern that informs this book. This is a history of Ireland since 1780.

The material is arranged in twelve chapters. The first eleven are largely narrative. Chapter 1 traces the effects of the French Revolution in Ireland. Chapter 2 recalls the rising of 1798, which was the French revolutionary spirit at large in the land accompanied by some other, older indigenous forces that did not sit easily with it. The failure of the rising led, not to an Irish republic, but to a full union with the metropolitan British state. The old colonial parliament in Dublin liquidated itself. Chapter 3 looks at the first serious attempt to subvert the union settlement through the movement led by Daniel O'Connell, the most protean figure in Irish history. The next chapter is a survey of various developments in Ireland immediately before the Great Famine, some of which were of prime importance for the future. Chapter 5 is an account of the Famine itself, the greatest human crisis in Irish history and a truly transfiguring event: one might easily divide the whole period of this book into two, pre- and post-Famine. Chapter 6 reviews the slow recovery from the Famine and also the decisive separation of Ulster from the other three provinces through its embrace of the Industrial Revolution, compounding older patterns of difference. Chapter 7 sees Irish nationalism in embryo under Parnell, the natural successor to O'Connell. The fall of Parnell produced an ennui with parliamentary politics that sought an outlet in cultural politics and the arts. Chapter 8 surveys this period, which ends with the revolutionary events of 1912–23, the subject of Chapter 9. The last two narrative chapters look first at the introverted twin states of partitioned Ireland and then at the seismic events in both parts of the island since the 1960s.

The final chapter takes the form of an essay, in which a series of themes is discussed and elaborated. It attempts to suggest contexts, continuities and disjunctions in the narrative that has preceded it.

No work of history is ever complete. It is not the job of the historian to propose neat endings, or to assume that the story – like a work of fiction – must be driven from the start towards the inevitable and only possible ending. Human affairs are full of random uncertainties, of roads not taken, of unexplored possibilities. There was, for instance, nothing inevitable about the Famine. As one of the most distinguished historians of that awful tragedy has concluded, it is possible to conclude that Ireland was simply very unlucky. The Famine hit at the worst possible moment, when the population was at its height but before an antidote had been discovered for the infestation. It was neither inevitable nor providential. And neither is anything else in this or any other history.

Richard Killeen
Dublin
August 2006

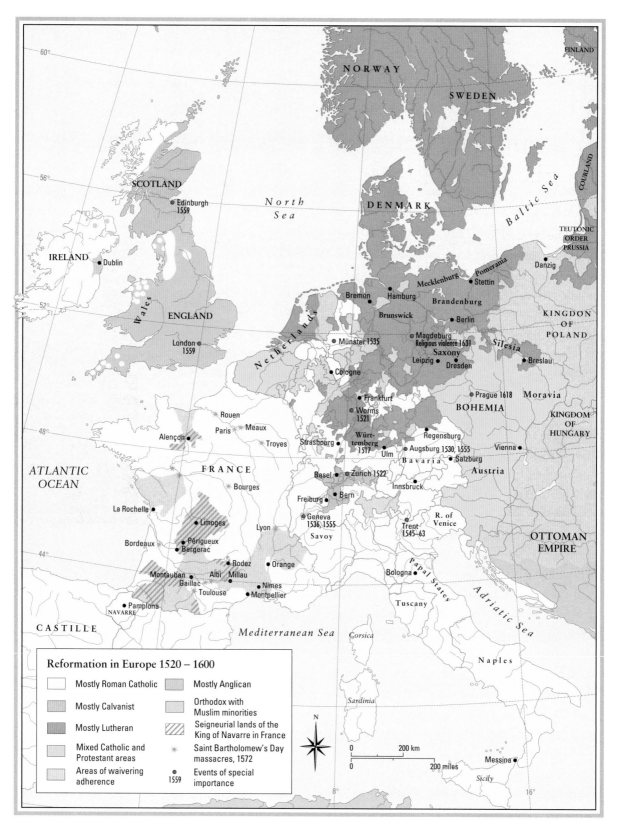

Reformation in Europe 1520 – 1600

Mostly Roman Catholic

Mostly Calvinist

Mostly Lutheran

Mixed Catholic and Protestant areas

Areas of waivering adherence

Mostly Anglican

Orthodox with Muslim minorities

Seigneurial lands of the King of Navarre in France

Saint Bartholomew's Day massacres, 1572

1559 Events of special importance

CHAPTER 1

A WORLD DESTROYED

Ancient Régime Ireland and the French Revolution 1780–97

In the eleventh century, Christian Europe divided east and west – never to be reunited – between the Latin and Orthodox churches. In the early sixteenth century, the Latin west further splintered at the Reformation. This seismic event, creating the twin poles of Catholicism and Protestantism, established the basic political fault lines for the continent for centuries. In Germany, where the two confessions met head to head, the Thirty Years War (1618–48) was the most destructive conflict in Europe prior to 1914.

Confessional allegiance was a mark of political loyalty. Until modern times, states found it almost impossible to accommodate dissenting religious minorities: thus what seem to us almost inexplicable actions made a certain contemporary sense. The expulsion of Muslims and Jews from Spain after 1492; the on-off toleration and persecution of French Huguenots; the witch hunt against Catholics in Elizabethan England: all were designed to protect the integrity of the royal state by ensuring religious conformity. The passions lying dormant in religious controversy were correctly recognised as a threat to the cohesion of the state itself. The Thirty Years War was eloquent testimony to the destructive potential of religious disputes.

This assumption – remote from modern sensibility, unless one recalls the ideological polarities of the Cold War – informed much of English thinking about Ireland in the pre-modern period, by which I mean the period from the Reformation to 1780. From the time of Henry VIII – and more decisively, from the reign of his daughter Elizabeth I (1558–1603) – England chose the Protestant path.

Ireland was part of the domain of the English crown. From 1541 it was established as a separate kingdom, having been a mere lordship for the previous 350 years. In all that time, it shared a common monarch with England. But Ireland resisted the Reformation and remained substantially Catholic. The biggest single problem for England was how the dominant Protestant state was to accommodate its Catholic sister kingdom. From the time of Elizabeth until at least 1815, England was successively opposed by the two

Upon the death of Mary in 1558, Elizabeth became Queen of England. During her reign, English rule was gradually extended into all four provinces of Ireland but the Protestant Reformation failed to win more than a small following.

great Catholic continental powers, Spain and France, in a series of wars that at times threatened its very independence. Inevitably, the necessity of securing Ireland and denying a friendly western beachhead to an invading Catholic enemy loomed large in the minds of London policy makers. English fears of the Irish back door were neither hysterical nor misplaced.

This made it essential that Ireland be governed in the interests of English security. After the confused series of wars that dominated the Tudor and Stuart eras, it seemed as if the Protestant interest in Ireland had finally triumphed in 1691 at Aughrim, the most decisive battle in Irish history. It meant the defeat of King James II, the last Catholic King of England, by his son-in-law William III and with it the defeat of the Catholic interest in Ireland itself.

For most of the eighteenth century, Ireland was ruled by a tiny Anglican elite – probably no more than 10 per cent of the population. The ascendancy, as it was later known, was not simply a colonial elite. All ancien regime governments were tiny elites: nowhere in Europe was there any notion of popular sovereignty or majority rule, ideas that for most of human history had been thought synonymous with mob rule and anarchy. Members of the ascendancy thought of themselves as local grandees governing in the king's name, just as their equivalents did in Northumberland or Bavaria or Languedoc. At the same time, it was plain that the ascendancy were – as many of them saw themselves – the English in Ireland. Most ascendancy families had been settled in Ireland following the Cromwellian confiscations of Catholic lands in the 1650s. As such, they had many of the qualities of a colonial garrison. The ascendancy was never quite sure what it was. Was it merely the natural ruling class of a separate kingdom? Or a peripheral elite at the margin of a larger Anglo-Irish world? Or a colonial pro-consular bridgehead?

The ascendancy was exclusively Anglican, that is adherents of the Church of Ireland by law established. The Church of Ireland had been established in the 1530s as a sister to the Church of England, with whom it shared many characteristics. It was Lutheran rather than Calvinist in structure, retaining an episcopal diocesan system. Whereas the Church of England has always conducted an unending internal dialogue between its High and Low Church wings – the former emphasising the inheritance from medieval Catholicism, the latter insisting on a more vigorous assertion of Reformation values – the Church of Ireland has traditionally been determinedly

Low Church. This is understandable: its self-image was that of a Protestant island in a sea of popish error. The easy-going tolerance of the English High Churchmen was a luxury the Church of Ireland could seldom afford.

The majority of the Irish population outside Ulster was Roman Catholic. This Catholic population was not an ethnic monolith. Its two tributary streams were the Old English and the Gaelic Irish. The Old English Catholics were the descendants of Anglo-Norman settlers from the twelfth and thirteenth centuries. They were similar in kind to other recusant groups at the margins of English life in Reformation times: there were similar patterns of resistance to the Reformation in Northumberland, Lancashire and corners of East Anglia. The Old English dominated life in provincial towns and were generally most numerous in the south and east of the island.

The other principal Catholic element was the Gaelic population. These were the descendants of the Celtic peoples who had first settled Ireland from 250 BC onwards, obliterating all trace of the aboriginal peoples they had displaced and establishing a cultural and linguistic homogeneity over the entire island. This homogeneity was disturbed first by the Vikings in the eighth century; then by the Normans in the twelfth; and more thoroughly and, from the Gaelic perspective, disastrously by the Protestant colonists and governors (the New English) in the sixteenth and seventeenth. The New English enterprise culminated in the Cromwellian land confiscations – in which the Old English lost more than the Gaels, simply because they had more to lose – and the creation of the land-owning class that in time became the ascendancy.

A shared confessional allegiance gradually drove the Old English and the Gaels together in what was sometimes an uncomfortable alliance against the common Protestant enemy. To the English eye, the division between Gaels and Old English was a distinction without a difference. Cromwell in the 1650s was the first person to treat all Irish Catholics as an undifferentiated unity regardless of their remote ethnic origins. Cromwell represented the temporary ascendancy of the most radical Calvinist strand in the English Protestant tradition. He identified Irish Catholics as a disloyal and rebellious fifth column which had tripped off a series of confused uprisings in the 1640s. Having pacified Ireland in a stunning military campaign, he dispossessed all Catholic landowners in the provinces of Leinster and Munster and removed them to Connacht, west of the River Shannon. The lands thus forfeit were settled instead by English parvenus, who had either fought in the army or lent money to the regime to finance the war. These New English – Protestant to a man – were the first generation of what later became known as the ascendancy.

Oliver Cromwell, ruthless general, country gentleman, devoted father and Puritan zealot. He came to Ireland determined to stamp out military resistance to government authority, to wreak vengeance for the massacres of 1641, and to secure the Protestant interest in Ireland.

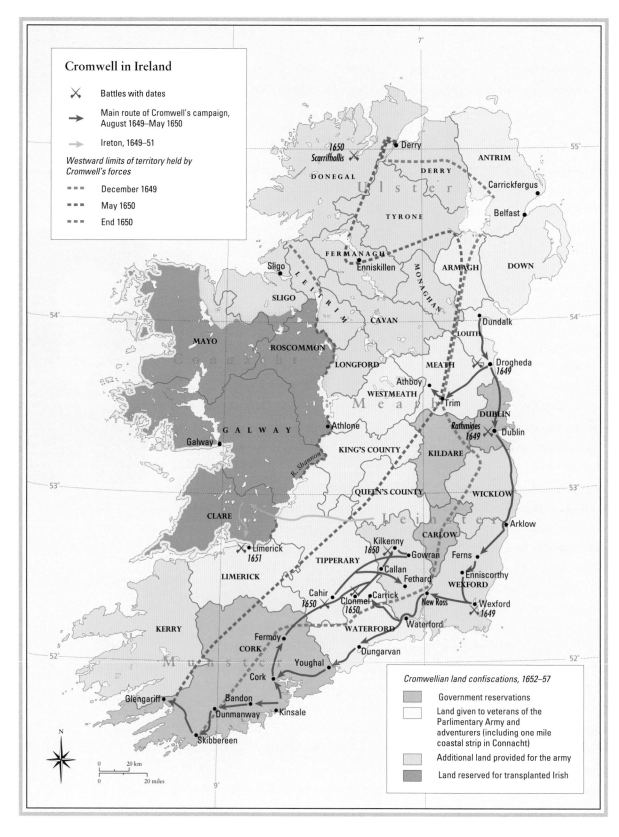

Cromwell in Ireland

X Battles with dates

→ Main route of Cromwell's campaign,
   August 1649–May 1650

→ Ireton, 1649–51

*Westward limits of territory held by
Cromwell's forces*

--- December 1649
--- May 1650
--- End 1650

Cromwellian land confiscations, 1652–57

Government reservations

Land given to veterans of the
Parlimentary Army and
adventurers (including one mile
coastal strip in Connacht)

Additional land provided for the army

Land reserved for transplanted Irish

Ulster had already been settled following an earlier war. After the defeat of the Ulster Gaelic lords in 1603, their lands were declared forfeit to the crown and were 'planted' by settlers from England and Scotland. All were Protestant. But there was a difference: whereas England had opted for a broadly Lutheran model, Scotland had unambiguously embraced Calvinism. These two great fault lines in Protestantism created many tensions both within England and between England and Scotland. In Ulster, however, the Presbyterians or Calvinists were a majority among the new settlers. Like the Catholics, they were excluded from the gilded circle of the Anglican elite. In fairness, the degree of exclusion was less – they were Protestant, after all – but the Anglicans had every reason to hold them in suspicion.

If Catholicism represented the enemy without in the form of France, Presbyterianism represented a version of the enemy within. For it was the Calvinist element within the Church of England that had prosecuted the English civil war of the 1640s; that had cut off the king's head; and that had presided over the unloved experiment in Puritan government under Cromwell. Moreover, it was the descendants of the English Puritans who settled North America in disproportionate numbers and who inflicted a humiliating defeat on the English crown by successfully seceding from English control and establishing the independence of the United States. When the story of modern Ireland begins in the 1790s, this was a thrillingly recent event.

Anglican suspicion of Presbyterians was not just theological. They disliked the levelling ideas associated with Calvinism in general: the absence of hierarchy in church government; the governance of the church by elected elders and assemblies. It smacked all too much of a kind of democracy and popular sovereignty. So while not disadvantaged as much as Catholics, the Presbyterians had definite grievances. They were obliged to pay tithes to the Church of Ireland; they felt oppressed by Anglican landlords, and in the eighteenth century many voted with their feet by emigrating to North America. There, they were known as the Ulster-Scots: ferocious, flinty frontiersmen who retained all their Calvinist fervour in their new wilderness.

The French Revolution of 1789 announced the birth of the modern world. The event was celebrated widely in Ireland, not least in Belfast. For the levelling Presbyterians of Ulster, the French Revolution meant the overthrow of tyranny and superstition. The fundamental importance of the French Revolution lay in its assertion of popular sovereignty. The people, not the monarch, were now to be the supreme sovereign power. Authority flowed upward from the people of the nation rather than downward through the king from God. Thus the nation state replaced the royal state. In the place of the king's domain, the underlying assumption was that all the citizens of the

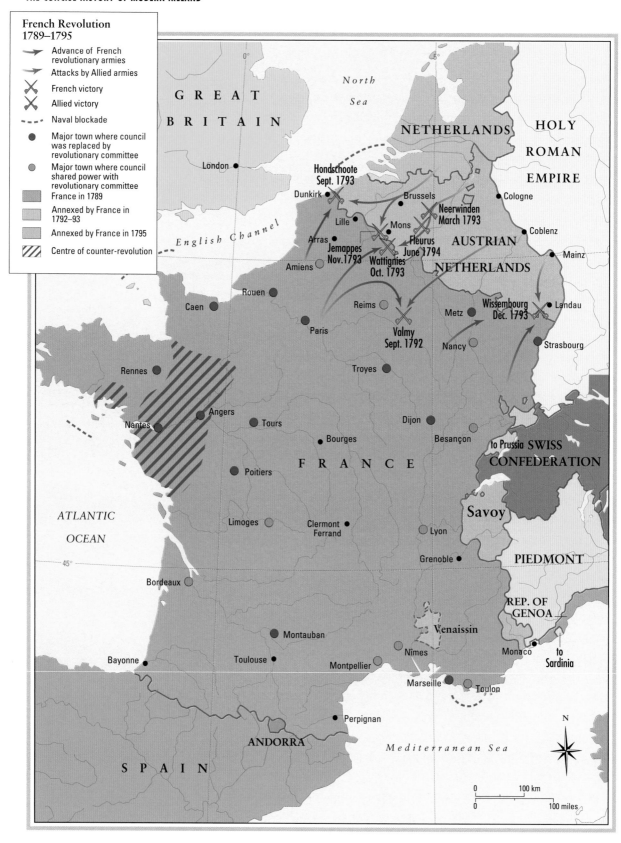

French Revolution
1789–1795

→	Advance of French revolutionary armies
→	Attacks by Allied armies
✕	French victory
✕	Allied victory
- - -	Naval blockade
●	Major town where council was replaced by revolutionary committee
●	Major town where council shared power with revolutionary committee
	France in 1789
	Annexed by France in 1792–93
	Annexed by France in 1795
▨	Centre of counter-revolution

state were stakeholders in a collective enterprise. That enterprise was called the nation and the force of collective will that drove it was nationalism. Nationalism – the assertion that a nation must have its own state grounded in popular sovereignty – is one of the most revolutionary political ideas in world history.

In 1791, the Society of United Irishmen was formed in Belfast. The three principal founders were Samuel Neilson, a Presbyterian who started life as a draper, became a newspaper proprietor and later a revolutionary; Thomas Russell, an Anglican ex-army officer and first librarian of the Linenhall Library in Belfast; and Theobald Wolfe Tone, a Dublin Anglican barrister and pamphleteer. A sister society was soon established in Dublin. The United Irishmen's declared purpose was to create a non-sectarian version of Irish identity in which confessional allegiance would not matter. Instead citizenship, the shared sense of identity in a civic society, would be the governing principle.

REGIMENTS IRLANDAIS

The United Irishmen were Irish but not always united. Some merely wanted parliamentary reform within the existing system, others – influenced by the quickening events in France and the outbreak of the revolutionary wars – an outright overthrow of the system and the establishment of an independent Irish republic. The longer the 1790s went on, the more the republican radicals made the running.

The 1790s was the crucible of modern Ireland. That means two things. First, novel ideas and movements developed that could not have flourished under the ancien régime and were implicitly hostile to it. Of these, nationalism and popular sovereignty were the most obvious. Second, however, counter-revolutionary forces developed with strong ancien régime continuities. They proved extraordinarily durable. Of these, the most important was the Orange Order.

Irish Volunteers in French service.

The order was formed in Co. Armagh in 1795, following a sectarian affray known as the Battle of the Diamond. In this, a Protestant faction called 'the Peep o' Day Boys' scored a victory over a Catholic agrarian secret society called the Defenders. These factions were determinedly traditional and confessional, their causes and concerns a world removed from the educated idealists of the United Irishmen. Following the Boys' victory, they withdrew to a pub in Loughgall, Co. Armagh and formed the Orange Order. From the start, the Orange was assertively Protestant, lower class, violent, and inveterately hostile to Catholics. It is significant that it drew most of its early support from the Church of Ireland rather than the Presbyterians, many of whom were much more attracted to French republicanism than Irish confessionalism.

The ancien régime powers of Europe were terrified by the French Revolution. By 1792, the first of a series of military coalitions against revolutionary France had mobilised against the upstart republic. At first, it simply comprised Austria and Prussia but between them they were sufficiently potent to carry the war onto French soil and to threaten Paris itself. But on 20 September 1792, the cannonade at Valmy saved the French Revolution. Coalition troops under the command of the Duke of Brunswick were scattered by an artillery barrage from a hastily assembled French volunteer army. Under their commander, Dumouriez, they consolidated their victory at Jemappes, swept the coalition forces out of north-eastern France, annexed what is now Belgium, threatened the southern Netherlands and occupied parts of the Rhineland including Mainz. In January of the following year, the king and queen – Louis XVI and Marie Antoinette – went to the guillotine. Great Britain joined the coalition. Britain was to be at war with France intermittently for the next twenty-three years.

The war transformed things in Ireland. It further radicalised many in the United Irishmen. By 1794, mere parliamentary reform was no longer enough: some were now demanding universal male suffrage, a republic and separation from Britain. The government in London responded in new ways as well. First, they persuaded the Dublin administration to pass a limited measure of parliamentary reform in Ireland, allowing some Catholics the vote for the first time. Some other civil disabilities were also removed. Ascendancy Ireland – both at the Castle and the parliament house – had grave reservations about the Catholic Relief Act of 1793 but it was forced through because Britain's strategic necessity in wartime demanded it. It needed a quiescent Catholic population and calculated that the most practical way to achieve this goal was to buy off the Catholic elite as best it could. In 1795, it ensured that the Irish parliament responded positively to a request from the Irish Catholic hierarchy to establish a national seminary for the training of diocesan clergy. Traditional clerical seminaries in France – and in lands threatened by French arms – were now off limits to Irish priests, so the establishment of St Patrick's College, Maynooth, just west of Dublin, answered an urgent need. That it was sponsored by the Irish parliament and encouraged by London was a mark of how changed times were. Any residual sectarian animus – and there was still plenty of that about – now had to yield to pragmatic necessity.

The British had either made a shrewd calculation or they had stumbled on what was to prove a major fault line in Irish nationalism. Right from the start, from the turbulence of the 1790s, there was a tension – to put it no stronger than that – between the clerical and the secular wings of nationalism. The secular wing had strong roots among disaffected Protestants. They regarded Catholicism as a farrago of superstition, doomed to extinction in the age of enlightenment. This attitude was especially marked among Ulster Presbyterians like William Drennan, but it was a sentiment shared even by a mild-mannered southern Anglican like Wolfe Tone. It was a commonplace of liberal Protestantism. To Drennan, Tone and all the rest, the French Revolution meant the scattering of every form of obscurantism, including Catholicism.

The Catholic hierarchy of Ireland, rather obviously, did not agree. Or rather, they drew a similar conclusion from the evidence before them while detesting what they saw. For the bishops, the French Revolution was the Antichrist. In contrast to the untravelled provincial Protestants, they knew the continent well. There was a network of thirty Irish Catholic colleges and seminaries across Europe in which the high command of the eighteenth-century church had been educated. The influence of these colleges had been critical in arresting the spread of Protestantism in Ireland itself. By providing Irish Catholicism with a supply line of educated clergy, they ensured the Church's astonishing recovery from the era of the Penal Laws. It is a remarkable fact that as early as the 1760s, every Catholic diocese in the country had its bishop in situ: the musculature of the church was strong.

THE

DECLARATION, RESOLUTIONS,

AND

CONSTITUTION,

OF THE

SOCIETIES OF UNITED IRISHMEN.

DECLARATION AND RESOLUTIONS.

IN the prefent great Æra of Reform, when unjuft Governments are failing in every quarter of Europe ; when Religious Perfecution is compelled to abjure her Tyranny over confcience ; when the Rights of Men are afcertained in Theory, and that Theory fubftantiated by Practice; when Antiquity can no longer defend abfurd and oppreffive Forms, againft the common Senfe and common Interefts of Mankind ; when all goverments are acknowledged to originate from the People, and to be fo far only obligatory, as they protect their Rights and promote their Welfare :— We think it our Duty, as Irifhmen, to come forward, and ftate what we feel to be our heavy Grievance, and what we know to be its effectual Remedy.

WE HAVE NO NATIONAL GOVERNMENT. — We are ruled by Englifhmen, and the Servants of Englifhmen, whofe Object is the Intereft of another Country ; whofe Inftrument is Corruption, and whofe ftrength is the Weaknefs of IRELAND ; and thefe Men have the whole of the Power and Patronage of the Country, as Means to feduce and fubdue the Honefty of her Reprefentatives in the Legiflature. Such an extrinfic Powers, acting with uniform Force, in a Direction too frequently oppofite to the true Line of our obvious Interefts, can be refifted with Effect folely by the *Unanimity, Decifion,* and *Spirit* in the *People*,—Qualities which may be exerted moit legally, conftitutionally, and efficacioufly, by that great Meafure, effential to the Profperity and Freedom of Ireland—AN EQUAL REPRESENTATION OF ALL THE PEOPLE IN PARLIAMENT.

The Constitution of the United Irishmen.

The bishops therefore had first-hand experience of ancient régime Europe and some clergy had first-hand experience of the Revolution itself. Indeed, most observant Irish Catholics, clerical or lay, who witnessed the Revolution disliked what they saw. Daniel O'Connell was the best-known example but not the only one. For loyal Catholics, the radical anti-clericalism of French republicanism could only be offensive.

Yet the emerging language of Irish nationalism was assuming a republican grammar. And this in a country where the vast majority of the population was Catholic and inhabited a mental world in which confessional allegiance was the primary badge of communal identity. This was a dichotomy little remarked on in the 1790s but which was full of significance for the future. Irish nationalism would evolve into the political project of the massed ranks of Irish Catholics. But which was to come first, the Irishness or the Catholicism?

While mollifying the secular and clerical Catholic elite, the London government and the Irish administration determined to crack down on republicanism. A spy called William Jackson betrayed many members of the Dublin United Irishmen, as a result of which the society was suppressed in the capital. It went underground. Among those betrayed by Jackson was Wolfe Tone.

He was lucky to escape the scaffold. Instead, he was allowed to go to the United States, from where he subsequently made his way to France. There, he used his considerable charm and powers of persuasion to press the Irish revolutionary cause on the French government. It was quite a performance. He had no pre-existing connections in the French capital except for an acquaintance with James Monroe, the American ambassador and later fifth President of the United States. He was often lonely but proved to be single-minded in a way that would have surprised the many in Ireland who regarded him as a lightweight. Monroe opened doors for him with the French Directory and eventually he met Lazare Carnot, its most important and impressive member. Carnot, famously dubbed 'the organiser of victory', was a supremely gifted administrator. More to the point, he was also Minister of War.

Wolfe Tone, as drawn in 1798 for Walkers Hibernian Magazine.

The result was a massive naval invasion force which gathered at Brest in December 1796. Comprising 43 warships and almost 15,000 crack troops under the command of General Lazare Hoche, it slipped past the Royal Navy convoys sent to engage it and reached Bantry Bay just before Christmas. On board the *Indomptable*, an 80-gun ship of the line, dressed in the uniform of a French officer, was Theobald Wolfe Tone.

Bantry Bay is on the south-west coast of Ireland. The French fleet sailed into this magnificent inlet and immediately struck disaster. The prevailing wind, from the south west, should have blown them up the bay to permit them to berth and disembark the troops. Had they done so, the road to Cork lay open. Cork was the principal city of the south and it and the countryside around was poorly defended. The French would have taken it easily. But they never got ashore.

The wind suddenly swung around to the east and blew a gale. The French could not land. Tone expressed his frustration by saying that he could have thrown a biscuit onto the shore, so close were they. On Christmas Eve, Hoche gave the order to cut and run and the remnants of the expedition limped back to Brest. It had been an astonishing escape for England. The 'Protestant wind' that had scattered the Spanish Armada and blown William III across the channel at the time of the Glorious Revolution seemed to have blown again.

The near miss galvanised the government both in London and in Dublin. Pre-emptive defensive meas-ures were taken across the country against suspected United Irishmen and their associates. This often involved great brutality on the part of crown forces. But it seemed to have worked when the leadership of the Leinster Directory of the United Irishmen was betrayed by spies in March 1798. The leading revolutionary figures in Dublin were captured. One, the charismatic Lord Edward Fitzgerald – a younger son of the Duke of Leinster – was fatally injured.

A United Irish badge.

The presence of a duke's son in the inner councils of a revolu-tionary organisation was evidence of the danger to the government posed by the United Irishmen. The Society was by now genuinely revolutionary, espousing a republican civic order in which traditional distinctions of reli-gion, class and caste would be sunk in a common citizenship. The demand was for a civic republic, completely independent of Britain.

With the capture of the Dublin leadership, it seemed that the United Irishmen had been beaten before they had begun. It was not so. Within two months, the bloodiest conflict in Irish history would break out.

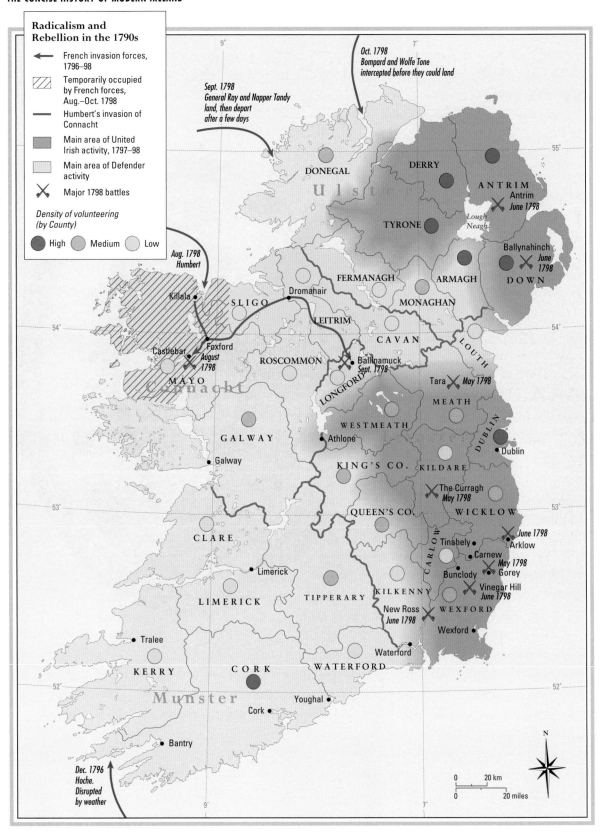

Radicalism and Rebellion in the 1790s

French invasion forces, 1796–98

Temporarily occupied by French forces, Aug.–Oct. 1798

Humbert's invasion of Connacht

Main area of United Irish activity, 1797–98

Main area of Defender activity

Major 1798 battles

Density of volunteering (by County)

High   Medium   Low

Oct. 1798
Bompard and Wolfe Tone intercepted before they could land

Sept. 1798
General Ray and Napper Tandy land, then depart after a few days

Aug. 1798
Humbert

DONEGAL

Ulster

DERRY

ANTRIM
Antrim June 1798

Lough Neagh

TYRONE

Ballynahinch June 1798

DOWN

FERMANAGH

ARMAGH

MONAGHAN

Killala

SLIGO

Dromahair

LEITRIM

CAVAN

LOUTH

Castlebar

Foxford August 1798

Ballinamuck Sept. 1798

ROSCOMMON

LONGFORD

Tara May 1798

MEATH

MAYO

Connacht

WESTMEATH

DUBLIN

GALWAY

Athlone

KING'S CO.

KILDARE

Dublin

Galway

The Curragh May 1798

WICKLOW

QUEEN'S CO.

June 1798
Arklow

CLARE

CARLOW

Tinahely

Carnew

Limerick

May 1798
Gorey

Bunclody

Vinegar Hill June 1798

KILKENNY

WEXFORD

LIMERICK

TIPPERARY

New Ross June 1798

Wexford

Tralee

KERRY

CORK

WATERFORD

Waterford

Munster

Youghal

Cork

Bantry

Dec. 1796
Hoche. Disrupted by weather

N

0   20 km
0   20 miles

CHAPTER 2

UNEASY UNION
The 1798 Rising and the
Act of Union 1798–1820

In fact, the gloves had been off for some time. Ever since the Bantry Bay near miss in December 1796, the Irish administration had been thoroughly frightened. Their apprehensions were shared by loyalists throughout the island. Frightened people find it easy to over-react, and so it was in 1797 and early 1798. The administration was determined to root out rebellion and conspiracy and it had at its disposal the means to do so. The Militia and the Yeomanry were deployed.

The Militia had been formed in 1793, at the time when Britain joined the First Coalition against the French. It was the latest of a series of such bodies that dated back to 1666. It was a full-time civilian reserve that could be mobilised for emergency or supplementary military duties. (It was the remote historical antecedent of the Territorial Army.) Although Catholics were admitted to the lower ranks, it was overwhelmingly Protestant and its officer corps completely so. In order to minimise the potential for neighbourly feuds and score-settling, the Militia were usually deployed away from the locations where they were raised.

A fanciful reconstruction of a United Irish gathering.

No such scruple was employed in the case of the Yeomanry, formed in 1796 at a time of rising tension. The 'Yeos', notorious in popular memory, were a part-time civilian reserve deployed specifically to harass the United Irishmen in their localities. As such, they anticipated the notoriously sectarian B Specials in Northern Ireland from the 1920s to the 1970s, underlying one of the more dismal continuities in British rule in Ireland – one grounded in an absence of legitimacy.

Between them, the Militia and the Yeomanry could turn out 70,000 men by early 1798. The 1790s had also brought the passage of a series of law-and-order enactments in parliament, with a predictable increase in charges brought against suspects. The conviction rate did not match the prosecution rate, however: local juries, even when not intimidated (and many were) were slow to find against neighbours with whom they must frequently have shared sympathies.

Habeas corpus was suspended in late 1796. The administration's counter-insurgency campaign now moved progressively into an extra-legal course. There was wholesale intimidation and harassment of radicals, republicans, United Irishmen and any others believed to be subversive of the state. The army was more freely employed, supported by the Militia and the Yeomanry. Political societies and meetings were broken up; troops were billeted on suspect households; some houses were simply burned down *pour décourager les autres*. Pitch-capping was a particularly brutal and well remembered torture. The suspect had a piece of paper soaked in pitch fastened to the scalp and set alight. Other rough methods included half-hanging and the cutting off of a suspect's earlobes, a practice known as 'shearing'.

The person principally responsible for this reign of terror was a bluff English officer, General Gerard Lake. He was brave: no one ever doubted his courage and competence. He had distinguished himself in the American war (not a distinguished time for British military competence generally) and was to do so again in India when his time in Ireland was over. He was freely encouraged by the Irish administration to get on with pacifying Ulster by whatever means it took to get the job done, without regard to legal niceties or the troubled scruples of local magistrates. For this kind of work, Lake was just the man.

He was a recognisable military type, decisive and logical within a blinkered perspective. Ulster in late 1796, when Lake assumed command of the army there, was in a state of extreme civil unrest. Quite where the United Irish movement ended and the Defenders – the much older agrarian secret society for the communal protection of Catholics – began was anyone's guess. Moreover, the foundation of the Orange Order in 1795 had mobilised lower-class Protestant resentment, much of which found formal expression through Orange membership of the Militia and Yeomanry.

The ever-rising climate of fear, paranoia and suspicion was fuelled by a series of sectarian affrays centred on the cockpit of Co. Armagh. As early as 1791, a Presbyterian clergyman in South Armagh, reporting a particularly horrifying attack by a Catholic mob on a local Protestant school teacher and his family, reported that 'the whole country for ten mile round is in absolute rebellion and confusion' and lamented the recrudescence of 'the same hereditary enmities handed down from generation to generation'. As the decade wore on, things got worse. When Lake took up his post, it seemed to him that his duty was not to separate two murderous sectarian factions, but to protect the integrity of the state by whatever means.

In effect, Lake and the military had to take sides against the overwhelmingly Catholic United Irishmen and Defenders. This he did with gusto, employing the methods already mentioned. Lake's 'dragooning of Ulster' was brutally effective. 'Nothing but terror will keep them in order', he claimed, as he introduced martial law and began a systematic combing of the province for arms. He was as brutal in his attacks on Presbyterian radicals and republicans as on Catholics. Indeed, while the latter were a threat to the civil peace the former – being the intellectual elite of the United Irishmen – were a more potent threat to the state. A number of Presbyterian clergy were executed: the most famous victim of this dragonnade was the Presbyterian William Orr. Lake even threatened to burn Belfast if that was what it would take.

The upshot of Lake's campaign was the near destruction of the United Irish movement in the northern half of the island. The movement had been stronger there than in the southern half. By March 1798, therefore, with the Leinster Directory of the United Irishmen captured or scattered and the movement in Ulster half broken, the Dublin administration must have felt that the crisis had been averted. In fact, it was about to reach its climax.

Although gravely weakened, the relatively decentralised structure of the United Irishmen saved the society from annihilation. Moreover, the surviving leadership decided that their best hope now lay in an early rebellion. There was no point in waiting for further French help that might never come, or would come too late. Nor was there any point in waiting supinely for Lake to come south and repeat his Ulster medicine there.

The 1798 rising broke out on the night of 23–24 May. Mail coaches leaving Dublin were intercepted, the signal for the rising to begin. The United Irishmen belied their name by being organised on county-by-county basis. Early outbreaks in the counties near Dublin were contained, but the rising in Co. Wexford – in the south-east corner of Ireland – was not. Co. Wexford rose on the afternoon of 26 May, as rumours of massacres and other atrocities in neighbouring counties began to filter through.

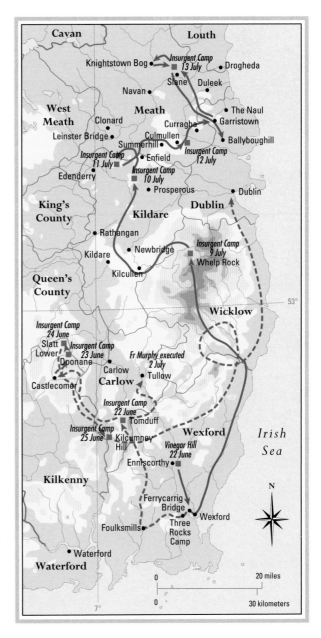

**The Long March
22 June–14 July**
(*after Stout*)
**The Routes of the
Wexford Rebels**

→ Roche and Fitzgerald

--▶ Fr Murphy and
Myles Byrne

■ Rebel encampment

The command structure of the United organisation in Wexford was interesting: it comprised some liberal Protestant landlords as well as well-to-do Catholic tenant farmers and some Catholic priests. Not all Protestants were pro-government; not all Catholics were for rebellion.

When the Wexford rising broke out, the county leadership understood itself to be part of a grand national plan. Its job was to secure the county and await orders. They held the county but the orders never came. The rebellion failed in the surrounding counties, just as it prospered briefly in Wexford. The rebels won a decisive victory against regular crown troops in an affray at Oulart Hill, almost in the middle of the county. In doing so, they demonstrated a degree of discipline and organisation not normally associated with irregular troops. Wexford, the county town, fell to the rebels on 30 May. They had the county, or most of it, but they were on their own.

The Battle of Vinegar Hill saw the final defeat of the 1798 Rising in County Wexford.

They quickly realised that their best hope lay in breaking into neighbouring counties and re-igniting the revolution there. This meant a push to the west, which meant taking New Ross, a market town on the upper tidal reaches of the River Barrow. On 5 June, the United troops laid siege to New Ross. In what was easily the bloodiest action of the rising, the fighting raged back and forth all day, often desperate hand-to-hand stuff in the narrow streets of the town. In the end, the rebels were repulsed.

develop into an overwhelmingly Catholic project. It was ironic, therefore, that most Catholic opinion in 1800 welcomed the Union. In the first place, it meant the end of the unreformed and corrupt parliament of the Protestant ascendancy. In the second place, it was to be accompanied by a measure of Catholic Emancipation. Locked in a deadly struggle with France, William Pitt, the British prime minister, recognised the need to avoid a disaffected population in Ireland. Catholics had suffered under a series of Penal Laws since the 1690s. Catholic political power was curbed by the denial of property rights; entry to parliament or the legal profession was barred; and Catholics could not keep their own schools. The relief measures now proposed would essentially grant Catholics full parliamentary rights in return for a government veto on Catholic

'Billy the Grinder': a contemporary cartoon of William Pitt rubbing British and Irish noses on the Union grindstone.

episcopal appointments. The Catholic hierarchy conducted discussions with the London government in this broad context.

It would be easier to grant full political rights to Catholics in the overall Protestant context of a union parliament. In a purely Irish context, however, Catholic political rights would be a direct threat to Protestant hegemony. This was a variation on Fitzgibbon's theme, although he was personally opposed to all concessions to Catholics. As things were to work themselves out, he was not alone.

The plan foundered on the inflexible opposition of the king. George III regarded such concessions as a violation of his coronation oath, which pledged to uphold the Protestant nature of the state. Like a lot of stupid people, it took a great deal to get an idea into the king's head but once there, there was no shifting it. The failure to couple Catholic Emancipation with the union was regarded as a betrayal by Irish Catholic opinion, one that blighted relations

The Entry of the Speaker into the Irish House of Commons in 1782 by Francis Wheatley.

between Catholics and the new order from the start.

The new regime meant that Ireland was no longer a separate kingdom but an integral part of the British state. In one respect, however, there was little change. The Irish administrative machinery remained not just a Protestant preserve, but increasingly an Orange one. The horrors of 1798 seized the imagination of many Irish Protestants, who did what people everywhere do when they feel threatened and vulnerable. They sought refuge in a more radical and defensive statement of their position. In the Protestant community, the ultras were able to say to the liberals: we told you so. And thus the ultras controlled the Castle in the early years of the union. The practical effect was to underscore the oppositional bitterness between Protestant and Catholic in Ireland. Liberal Protestants were pushed towards the margins of their own community. The prevailing temper of Irish Protestantism under the Union grew ever more defensive.

Meanwhile, in the first two decades of the new century, a sea-change was occurring among the Catholics which was to be the decisive social and intellectual shift in nineteenth-century Ireland. The idea of the modern Irish nation was being born.

The principles of republican government, independence and popular sovereignty had all been asserted in 1798. This was the work of a political elite, many of them Protestant radicals intoxicated by the revolutionary fervour coming from France. This new ideal of a civic order, indifferent to religion, was severely damaged by the sectarian outrages in Wexford. Its last aftershock, the failed insurrection of Robert Emmet in Dublin in 1803, also resulted in unintended tragedy. It was quickly snuffed out and was in fact little more than an affray, but one which claimed the life of Lord Kilwarden, the Lord Chief Justice, a notably liberal judge. The irony was that Kilwarden's birth name was Arthur Wolfe. He was a member of the family for whom Wolfe Tone had been named (Tone's father had been a tenant on the Wolfe estate) and he himself had used his influence to help save Tone's life back in 1794 when Tone's activities had been betrayed to the government.

After a speech from the dock that still resonates in Irish history, Robert Emmet was hanged.

In place of civic republicanism, the older tradition of Catholic self-consciousness re-asserted itself. But now it took new form. Ever since the Reformation, Catholics had felt themselves to be a distinct community. But in this they were little different from many such communities in Habsburg lands. The ethnic sub-groups gradually asserted their rights to national status, to a state of their own independent of the empire. Why the change? What was happening in the Irish Catholic community in the early nineteenth century?

First, the revolutionary idea of popular sovereignty had influenced even people who were otherwise hostile to the French Revolution. Second, an embryonic national consciousness began to form. Gaelic Ireland – to take the larger element in the Catholic community – had long had a cultural unity while being bitterly divided politically. Only as Catholics began to believe that what they had in common was paramount and what divided them was of little consequence did the community begin to develop a national self-consciousness. It is the key process in the birth of nationalism.

It is also a startlingly modern idea. In eighteenth-century Ireland, a Catholic in the Glens of Antrim felt no sense of common political purpose with a Catholic in Kerry or Clare. By the end of the 1820s, this sense of communal affinity was developing among Irish Catholics. By the 1880s, it was the most potent force in Irish life. Why did it happen, and why did it happen when it did?

First, there is the intellectual revolution: the idea of popular sovereignty which provided a template into which ideas that had hitherto been diffuse could now cohere.

Second, there is the rise of a Catholic middle class. This too is crucial. All nations require a leadership element to focus their emerging national consciousness. In every European case – in Poland, Bohemia, Hungary, Germany – the people who made the running were always the same: lawyers, doctors, professors, younger sons of minor gentry. These were educated people, ambitious but usually frustrated by institutional or political impediments to their advance. These impediments were invariably embedded deep in the structures of the old regime.

Third, there was the gradual destruction of distance which helped to create a sense of national as distinct from local community. Better roads and coach services and canals were a beginning, but above all it was the coming of the railways that made this possible. It made it possible to distribute goods and services nationally. It created a national press, because it facilitated the countrywide distribution of newspapers published in Dublin. By the second half of the century, there was a national community in the sense that matters of common national interest had a means of common expression. The Catholics of Antrim were no longer remote from those of Kerry: they no longer shared just a common culture, but now had common political aspirations as well. And the first of those aspirations was fair play for the Catholic community, which began with the demand for Catholic Emancipation. Later, nationalism demanded the repeal of the union; later, after the Famine, it recast this demand in the form of the home rule movement; finally, it asserted itself in arms and formulated the demand for full independence from Britain.

The self-conscious community of Irish Catholics began its life in the first two decades of the nineteenth century, in the era of Orange administrative dominance. The sense of betrayal over Catholic Emancipation went deep. It was this cause that became the focus of Catholic aspiration. Moreover, it found a leader and organiser of genius. His name was Daniel O'Connell.

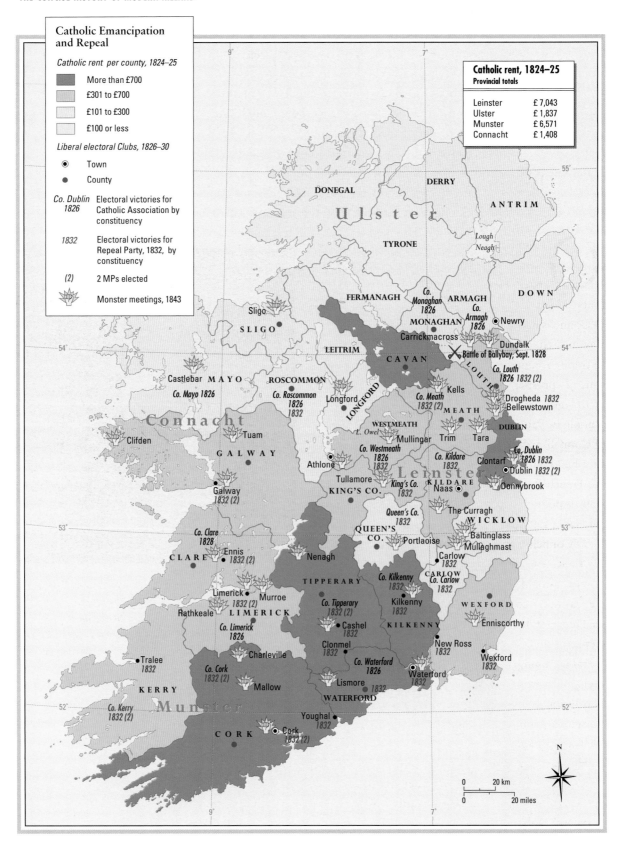

Catholic Emancipation and Repeal

Catholic rent per county, 1824–25

- More than £700
- £301 to £700
- £101 to £300
- £100 or less

Liberal electoral Clubs, 1826–30

- ◉ Town
- ● County

Co. Dublin 1826 — Electoral victories for Catholic Association by constituency

1832 — Electoral victories for Repeal Party, 1832, by constituency

(2) — 2 MPs elected

Monster meetings, 1843

Catholic rent, 1824–25 Provincial totals	
Leinster	£ 7,043
Ulster	£ 1,837
Munster	£ 6,571
Connacht	£ 1,408

CHAPTER 3

KING OF THE BEGGARS

Daniel O'Connell and the Birth of Nationalism 1820–30

O'Connell was the scion of a minor Gaelic aristocratic family from Co. Kerry. His background was classically part of that hidden Ireland of the ancien régime. The O'Connells had survived and prospered in a modest way in their remote coastal fastness, not scrupling to trade in smuggled goods if necessary. Like many sons of prosperous Catholics in eighteenth-century Ireland, the young Daniel was sent to the Jesuit schools in Saint-Omer and Douai to be educated. O'Connell arrived there in 1791 and witnessed at first hand enough of the violence associated with the French Revolution to give him a lifelong aversion to political violence in general. He later studied law in London.

O'Connell was a key figure – perhaps even the key figure – in the modernisation of Ireland, but in

Daniel O'Connell, known as 'The Liberator', was one of the most charismatic leaders of his generation and enjoyed a reputation as a libertarian that extended far beyond Ireland's shores.

his educational formation he was very much a product of the ancien régime. He was never comfortable with French revolutionary principles. He inclined to see French-style republicanism as an anti-clerical minority tyranny. His achievement, on the other hand, was to entail the mobilisation of an overtly confessional community – the Irish Catholics – at a time when that community was itself borrowing as much of the language and grammar of the French Revolution as it could comfortably absorb. The Irish Catholics had been a self-conscious community since the Reformation: after O'Connell it thought of itself as a nation.

He was one of the first generation of Catholics allowed to practice law under the terms of a Catholic Relief Act passed in 1793. He qualified in 1798, the year of rebellion. He was a member of a lawyers' reserve militia mobilised to defend Dublin against a threatened United Irish attack that never materialised. He went on to practice on the Munster circuit, made and spent fortunes and married happily.

He was drawn to political prominence from 1808 on by the veto controversy. The proponents of Catholic Emancipation assumed that – as at the time of the union – the Catholic hierarchy would concede to the British government a veto on Irish episcopal appointments as a quid pro quo for Emancipation. The demand for a veto of some sort had been there since the Catholic Church had started to emerge from the wilderness years of the Penal Laws in the last quarter of the eighteenth century with an institutional vigour that astonished and dismayed London. The proposed veto was intended to exercise at least some degree of negative control over the leadership of this potentially dangerous body. Moreover, it was the norm in many parts of Europe: the Protestant kings of Prussia exercised a veto over the appointment of bishops to the Catholic Church in Poland, for example.

The more radical, middle-class faction among Irish Catholic activists was unimpressed by Prussia or anywhere else. They were adamant in opposition to the veto. An older, more aristocratic leadership – both among the hierarchy and the laity – was open to the possibility but they were overborne. The controversy rumbled on all through the 1810s. In part, the anti-vetoists represented a generational change, in part a class one: what was significant was the exceptional vigour with which they argued for the absolutely free-standing autonomy of the Catholic community and its church.

This was part of the great change that was quietly transforming Irish Catholicism. The aristocratic old order was prepared to accommodate itself to the state, however reluctantly, in a typically ancien régime way. The radicals were not. The passions aroused by this issue split Irish Catholics bitterly and made any united political action on Emancipation impossible until the wounds had healed in the 1820s.

The Catholic Church had suffered the disabilities of the Penal Laws for most of the eighteenth century. As we saw, it emerged into the new century in remarkably fine shape, considering the rigours of the old one. All the dioceses had bishops in residence, there were numerous priests, the Irish Church was in full communion with Rome and while many peasant practices persisted which the clergy deplored as superstitious, there was a movement towards doctrinal and liturgical orthodoxy which advanced steadily as time went on.

The church was strongest where the community was strongest. One of the striking things about the church in the early nineteenth century was its regional disparities. In the impoverished west of Ireland, it still remained a pre-modern peasant body. But in the south-east, in the rich river valleys and towns where the Old English Catholic middle class had survived the bad days in good

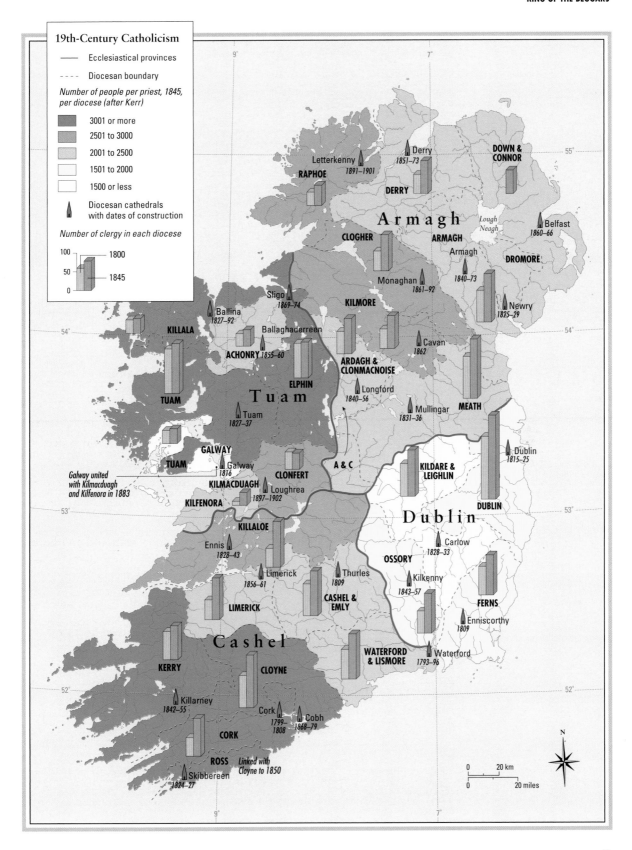

19th-Century Catholicism

— Ecclesiastical provinces
---- Diocesan boundary

Number of people per priest, 1845, per diocese (after Kerr)

- 3001 or more
- 2501 to 3000
- 2001 to 2500
- 1501 to 2000
- 1500 or less

Diocesan cathedrals with dates of construction

Number of clergy in each diocese

100
50
0

1800
1845

Letterkenny
RAPHOE
Derry
1851–73
DERRY
DOWN & CONNOR
Armagh
Lough Neagh
Belfast
1860–66
CLOGHER
ARMAGH
Monaghan
1861–92
Armagh
1840–73
DROMORE
Newry
1825–29
KILMORE
Sligo
1869–74
Ballina
1827–92
KILLALA
Ballaghaderreen
ACHONRY *1855–60*
Cavan
1862
ARDAGH & CLONMACNOISE
ELPHIN
TUAM
Tuam
1827–37
Tuam
1827–37
Longford
1840–56
Mullingar
1831–36
MEATH
GALWAY
Galway
1816
TUAM
Galway united with Kilmacduagh and Kilfenora in 1883
KILMACDUAGH
CLONFERT
Loughrea
1897–1902
A & C
KILDARE & LEIGHLIN
Dublin
1815–25
KILFENORA
KILLALOE
Ennis
1828–43
DUBLIN
Dublin
Carlow
1828–33
Limerick
1856–61
Thurles
1809
OSSORY
Kilkenny
1843–57
LIMERICK
CASHEL & EMLY
FERNS
Cashel
Enniscorthy
1809
KERRY
CLOYNE
WATERFORD & LISMORE
Waterford
1793–96
Killarney
1842–55
Cork
1799–1808
Cobh
1868–79
CORK
ROSS
Linked with Cloyne to 1850
Skibbereen
1824–27

0   20 km
0   20 miles

N

Ulster had a Protestant majority. It was not a united community. Tensions between members of the established Church of Ireland (Anglican), mainly of English descent, and the Presbyterians of Scots descent were very marked. The liberal impulse in Presbyterianism, with its instinct for democracy, had found expression in 1798. Although much chastened thereafter, it took a long time for this liberal Presbyterian tradition to die. But by 1830, it was increasingly under challenge.

Presbyterianism, with its highly literate congregations, was a fertile ground for theological disputation. In the first half of the nineteenth century, conservative and orthodox subscribers to the Westminster Confession of Faith – the foundation document of the Church of Scotland – gradually marginalised the so-called non-subscribers within Ulster. In broad political terms, it was a victory for conservatives and evangelicals over those of a more liberal, accommodating temper.

The one thing that united all Ulster Protestants, whether Church of Ireland or any shade of Presbyterian, was suspicion and dislike of Catholics. The antagonism ran long and deep, right back to original Plantation days and it had never abated. It was no coincidence that the swing to conservatism in Presbyterianism coincided with the growing advance of Catholic interests under O'Connell.

As part of his campaign to organise nationally, O'Connell looked towards Ulster. Like Connacht, but for different reasons, it was not nearly as promising territory as the southern provinces. There was no self-confident Catholic middle class around which a mass movement could form and which would provide leadership for it. Moreover, many among the Protestant majority were enthusiastic Orange partisans. The point was made with some vigour in September 1828.

O'Connell approved an initiative by one of his more maverick allies, Honest Jack Lawless, to try to extend the reach of the Catholic Association to Ulster. This initiative was known by the revealing title of 'the invasion of Ulster', Honest Jack's own formulation. He led a large crowd north but was repulsed by a formidable gathering of Orangemen in Ballybay, Co. Monaghan. It was the first town on the southern reaches of Ulster where Protestants felt confident enough to muster in serious numbers. Lawless wisely backed off. Humiliatingly, that was as far as things went for the 'invasion' force: in the face of the first concentrated Ulster Protestant resistance to a nationalist initiative, all they could do was to retreat.

It was a portent. Resistance – bringing weight of numbers to bear in concentrated form – became the essence of the Ulster Protestant position as the nineteenth century wore on. There were lots of Ulster Protestants; they were concentrated in a small area; they were not going anywhere and there was no shifting them.

By the 1830s, the broad pattern of modern Irish history was in place. The Catholic community had realised its collective self-image and embarked on its political project. It gradually absorbed the key French Revolutionary idea of popular sovereignty, but located it in the context of a much older indigenous tradition. What began as an agitation to relieve Catholic disabilities gradually developed first into a campaign for Irish autonomy within the United Kingdom and later into a demand for outright independence. But Ulster, with its local Protestant majority, was outside this process and antagonistic to it.

The advance of the Irish nationalist project is interesting. It was not unique in Europe but its methods were. The contrast with Polish nationalism makes the point nicely. The Poles had seen their country dismembered in the Three Partitions and divided between Russia, Prussia and the Habsburgs. Their nine-teenth-century nationalist movement found itself facing three states with no tradition of representative government. So the leadership of Polish nationalism embarked on what they called 'organic work': educating the people in their his-

Daniel O'Connell addressing a Monster Meeting, 1840s.

tory and folklore; artists and writers producing didactic work on Polish themes; economic development; movements for social cohesion.

The kind of people who led this organic work were from the same sort of social background as O'Connell's lieutenants in Ireland: people like Wyse, Sheil, Scully and Lawless. But where the Poles directed their energies to what might broadly be called cultural and economic development, the Irish chose politics.

They did so because the country of which they were a part, the United Kingdom, had one of the longest continuous traditions of representative government in Europe. Britain was no democracy – not yet – but it did possess representative institutions, of which the most important was the House of Commons. It meant that Irish nationalism had a representative forum in which to express itself from the start: from 1829 to 1914, the House of Commons in London was the focus of all constitutional nationalist effort.

In Poland, organic work represented the only nationalist alternative to insurrection. In Ireland, it was politics. From the beginning, Irish nationalism was about numbers and representation; it was about incremental change and the practical politics of the here and now; it was populist. Thus the emphasis on organisation and mobilsation, on ward politics, and the impatience with theory. Irish populist politics first developed under O'Connell. It was perfected later in the century under Parnell. It has been exported wherever the Irish diaspora has gone in numbers and has given the world, among other things, Tammany Hall and much of the Democratic Party in the USA; a significant element of the Labour Party and trade union movement in Britain; and a substantial part of the Labor Party and trade union movement in Australia.

All this made Irish nationalism unusual in a European context. In Ireland, politics came first and culture followed. In comparable continental countries, it tended to be the other way around. This may explain why, in the 1920s and '30s, so many of the new states in Europe turned towards various forms of authoritarian government , while Ireland – despite the bitterness of the civil war divide – did not. Politics had become second nature to Irish nationalists. With its internal logic of compromise, the political process provided the normal means of settling great public issues. When you have a legitimate parliament, you have no need for a Man on a White Horse.

Georgian doorway, Dublin.

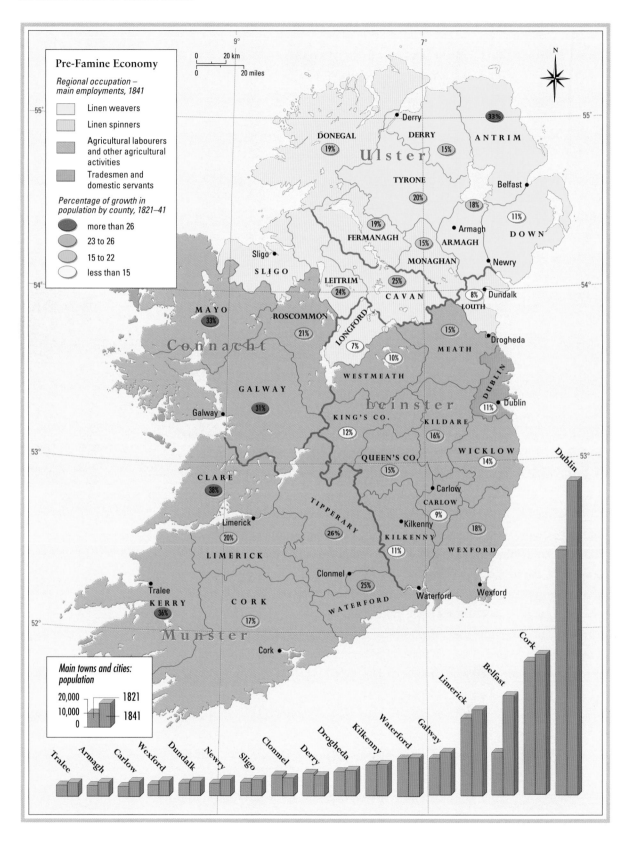

Pre-Famine Economy

Regional occupation –
main employments, 1841

- Linen weavers
- Linen spinners
- Agricultural labourers and other agricultural activities
- Tradesmen and domestic servants

Percentage of growth in
population by county, 1821–41

- more than 26
- 23 to 26
- 15 to 22
- less than 15

Main towns and cities:
population

20,000
10,000 · · · 1821
0 · · · 1841

CHAPTER 4

BEFORE THE FAMINE

Pre-Famine Ireland 1830–45

With Catholic Emancipation won, O'Connell entered parliament in London and gradually formed a loose group of supporters around him. This was not a party in any modern sense, with all the discipline and regimentation that term implies. Until the fall of Wellington and Peel in 1832, he had little parliamentary leverage. The accession of the Whigs to power in that year improved the position. O'Connell felt much closer to the Whigs, with their generally more liberal inclinations, than he possibly could to the royalist and reactionary Tories – especially given the latter's Orange allies in Ireland.

O'Connell reached an understanding with the Whigs which brought some immediate benefits. The long-running sore of the tithe question was set-tled. Tithes were a tax – notionally one-tenth of earnings – levied either in cash or kind for the upkeep of the clergy of the established Church of Ireland, whose congregations constituted barely 10 per cent of the entire Irish population. Tithes had always been resented and had been the proximate cause of sporadic campaigns of agrarian violence ever since the 1760s. These campaigns had escalated in the early 1830s, resulting in serious violence in the countryside. In general, attempts to enforce payment – or worse, to distrain goods for non-pay-ment, met with fierce resistance. The settlement of this issue removed one of the most potent sources of social unrest in Ireland.

Resistance to payment had been sporadic among Catholics since the 1760s. But in the period of heightened expectation following Catholic Emancipation, the sense of grievance turned to outright resistance. By the 1830s, almost two-thirds of the total income of the Church of Ireland came from tithes. Given this level of dependence, it was not an issue easily resolved. At the same time, it was a chronic source of grievance among people not in communion with the

Weighing potatoes, the staple of the agrarian community. Reliance on this single crop, together with the relative unsophistication of the Irish economy, left country people, particularly in the west, vulnerable to sudden change.

Church of Ireland, upon whom fell the main burden of payment. Moreover, from 1735 until 1823 pasturage was excluded from the scheme, which meant that the best land was exempt. Given the reality of land-holding patterns, this meant that wealthy members of the Church of Ireland paid less than their due proportion for the upkeep of their own church, while the principal burden fell on poorer Catholics and – in Ulster – Presbyterians.

The 'Tithe War' started in Graiguenamanagh, Co. Kilkenny in October 1830 when the cattle of the parish priest, Fr Martin Doyle – a relation of the formidable Bishop James Warren Doyle of Kildare & Leighlin – were distrained for non-payment. A campaign of non-payment first spread throughout South Leinster and Munster: once again, this critical region was in the van of modernisation. Eventually 22 of the 32 counties in Ireland were involved. Although formally a campaign of passive resistance, it inevitably turned violent.

The use of police and troops to distrain goods and livestock resulted in serious clashes. Fourteen people were killed at Newtownbarry (now Bunclody), Co. Wexford in 1831 when distrained cattle were sold off to settle unpaid tithes. In all, over 43,000 decrees were issued against defaulters, while Lord Gort claimed in 1832 that the anti-tithe campaign had resulted to date in 242 homicides; 1,179 robberies; 401 burglaries; 568 burnings; 280 cattle maimings; 161 assaults; 203 riots and 723 attacks on houses. The withdrawal of police and the Yeomanry from tithe enforcement duties in 1833 took much of the heat out of the situation, but by now the total arrears were more than £1 million. In effect, London gifted this sum to the Church of Ireland – an open acknowledgment that the traditional tithe system was no longer viable.

The tithe question was not settled by legislation until 1838, when O'Connell – who had kept his distance from the agitation while benefiting politically from it (he was not the last Irish nationalist to master this trick) – formed a proposal which would mean the state taking over responsibility for clerical payments, while a local tax would be levied in support of the newly formed Irish Constabulary. The proposal was broadly adopted by the government and although much watered down in the House of Lords was carried. The net effect was to convert the tithes into a rent charge, making them invisible. The hated tithe proctors, who had conducted the assessments and collected the tithes, disappeared from the land. With them went the visible reality of the problem itself.

Other reforms effected by the O'Connell-Whig alliance included the modernisation of the archaic system of municipal government by widening the franchise. Among other things, it allowed O'Connell to become the first Catholic lord mayor of Dublin for 150 years. A Poor Law enacted in 1838 provided a minimal structure of poor relief in what was still a desperately poor country. The English Poor Law system was extended to Ireland, ignoring the report of a Commission of Enquiry that had recommended a system for Ireland different from that of England and tailored more to the specific requirements of the country. The report's recommendations had included subsidised emigration for the very poorest as a way of relieving the ever-growing pressure on land caused by the rising population. In bypassing the report in this regard at least, the new Poor Law unwittingly ensured that within a decade famine would accomplish what legislation had avoided. O'Connell opposed the Poor Law Act, as much out of opportunism as conviction.

In the 1830s, the Irish administration was increasingly staffed by Catholics and liberal Protestants, weakening the Orange grip on Dublin Castle. The under-secretary (head of the Irish civil service), Thomas Drummond, famously reminded Irish landlords that 'property has its duties as well as its rights', not the sort of sentiment normally expected from the Castle. The establishment of the Irish Constabulary (the 'Royal' prefix came later, for services rendered in helping to put down the Fenian insurrection of 1867) and the Dublin Metropolitan Police in 1836 put Irish law enforcement on a modern footing.

With the possible exception of the coming of the railways (see below), nothing in Ireland in the 1830s was more important for the future than developments in education.

Many schools had been established in Ireland in the seventeenth and eighteenth centuries. Most were Protestant, but from the 1770s onwards the institutional revival of Catholic education began in earnest. In particular, new teaching orders of nuns were founded: the Presentation Order founded by Nano Nagle in Cork in 1776; the Irish Sisters of Charity founded by Mary Aikenhead in Dublin in 1815; the Sisters of Mercy founded by Catherine McAuley also in Dublin in 1831. The distribution of convents followed a now familiar pattern: clustered disproportionately in Munster and Leinster and much scarcer, at least until later in the century, in the north and west.

No single teaching order had a greater influence on nineteenth-century Ireland than the Christian Brothers. Once more, it was a product of the south-east quadrant, that early powerhouse of the institutional Catholic revival and by extension the crucible of Irish nationalism. Its founder, Edmund Ignatius Rice, had been born in Callan, Co. Kilkenny and had made a fortune in trade in Waterford as a young man. It was in that city that he opened the first Christian Brothers' school in 1802. The Christian Brothers became the educators of the sons of the Catholic poor, leaving the well-to-do to the Jesuits and others. They developed a disciplined and efficient approach to education. They were unsentimental and utilitarian: they regarded liberal humanism as a luxury

36. — Bianconi's Establishment.

Plate

Charles Bianconi came to Ireland from Italy in 1802 and established a coach system. Illustration of Bianconi's long cars.

their charges could ill afford, and something moreover which was offensive to their assertively Catholic, nationalist and – as time went on – Gaelic ethos.

Between all these different groups – and adding in the small private, fee-paying academies known as 'hedge schools' – there was an astonishing number of schools in Ireland by 1830, more than 10,000.

It was at this point that the government decided to establish a centralised national system. Under an act of 1831, an inter-denominational system of national schools was established. By the end of the nineteenth century, it had over a million pupils in almost 9,000 schools. But by then, the original inter-denominational ideal had long since been abandoned under pressure from the various churches, all of which wanted educational control of their own flocks. Denominational control of education was to persist all through the twentieth century, surviving the upheavals of revolution, independence and partition. It was carried into secondary education, as that system developed from the 1870s on, and even into the third-level sector. Trinity College Dublin was effectively a Protestant redoubt until the second half of the twentieth century. Its rival institution in the capital, founded in 1854, took the unambiguous name of the Catholic University; it was the remote ancestor of University College Dublin.

The real political action gradually came to focus not on these worthy reforms but on the larger constitutional issue. O'Connell launched a campaign for the repeal of the union of 1801 and the restoration of a parliament in Dublin. As the Whig government began to run out of steam, O'Connell reckoned that the potential for further reforming concessions was lessening by the day. With the return of the Tories under his old adversary Peel in 1841, the possibility vanished altogether.

O'Connell could therefore go for broke. He revived the methods that had stood him in such good stead in the Emancipation campaign: a national organisation, again leaning heavily on Catholic parish structures, complemented by fund raising and propaganda. To this potent brew he added a new element, the so-called 'monster meeting'.

Monster meetings were enormous public gatherings designed to show the formidable powers of organisation and control that O'Connell exercised over the people. They aimed to intimidate the government by sheer weight of numbers and by the implicit threat of public disorder on a massive scale. The meetings were organised at historic sites like Tara, Co. Meath and were always addressed by O'Connell.

Three things contributed to the failure of the repeal agitation. First, the Catholic hierarchy, although sympathetic, did not feel that repeal was as urgent a measure as Emancipation had been and did not throw their weight behind it to the same degree. Second, there was no body of sympathetic opinion in

England as there had been in the earlier campaign. Third, Peel exploited this knowledge to take a stand against O'Connell. When a monster meeting was announced for the Dublin suburb of Clontarf – site of a famous battle against the Vikings in 1014 – the government banned it. Fearing violence, which he loathed, O'Connell backed down and abandoned the meeting.

O'Connell briefly ended up in prison for his pains, although the conditions of his confinement were luxurious by the standards endured by most contemporary prisoners. More importantly, Clontarf was his Waterloo. This extraordinary man – brilliant, charismatic, vulgar, idealistic and cynical by turn – was finally a burnt-out case. He had been, as much as Parnell was to be forty years later, the 'uncrowned king of Ireland'. He had a European reputation as one who reconciled Catholicism and liberalism at a time when they were widely considered antipathetic. No sooner had he taken his seat at Westminster in 1829 than he took on the role of advocate for the cause of Jewish emancipation, in stark contrast to some later nationalists who never missed a chance to traduce O'Connell's memory while themselves cosying up to anti-Semites of every kind, not excluding the Third Reich. No Irish political figure since has enjoyed such an international celebrity. But now he was almost seventy. The magic was gone, the energy exhausted. By early 1847, overwhelmed by the disaster of the Famine, he stood for the last time in the House of Commons, barely audible and trembling in the grasp of the illness that would kill him before the year was out, begging alms from his enemy for a country that could no longer save itself. He begged the help of parliament, failing which he predicted that a quarter of the population of Ireland would be lost. He was right. Death and emigration saw to that. He did not live to see it.

The subsequent history of nationalist Ireland was a footnote to his achievement.

The first Irish railway, the Dublin & Kingstown, opened in December 1834. Within twenty years Dublin was connected to Belfast, Cork and Galway and there were a host of minor lines, radiating from these centres, either planned or already in place. The expansion of the Irish railway system continued up to the 1920s, when road transport began to supplant it.

The railways were crucial in the process of consolidating national consciousness. A journey like that from Dublin to Cork, which had taken two days by coach, was reduced to seven hours in 1849 and four hours by 1887. It was the greatest advance in mobility in human history and it led to all sorts of unanticipated consequences. It made possible the creation of a genuinely national press, by providing a distribution mechanism from Dublin. Thus, people at either end of the island could read the same newspaper on the same day. Likewise, it made the distribution of everything from tinned foods to beer easier and helped to create a national retail economy. It offered opportunities for leisure travel to tens of thousands to whom it was previously denied: the great Victorian 'watering places' – such seaside resorts as Bray, Tramore and Clifden – all owe their origins to the railway.

The railways annihilated distance, one of the characteristic features of the modern world. They helped to create a genuine national community. The new kind of nationalism ushered in by the French Revolution created the ideal of the nation state. But the railways gave it a physical reality. It is one thing to imagine the national community; it is another to realise it by travel. Before the railway, people in Co. Antrim had more contact with Argyll than with Kerry.

People gather at the Government Inspector's Office determined to take a ship for America. Engraving from the Illustrated London News.

Tyrone did not know Cork. Wexford and Donegal might have been in different countries. The railways connected people in a way that gave physical expression to their underlying cultural unity. Dublin's position as the nodal point in the railway system consolidated its position as a national rather than just a colonial capital.

The first reliable Irish census took place in 1841. It showed a population of

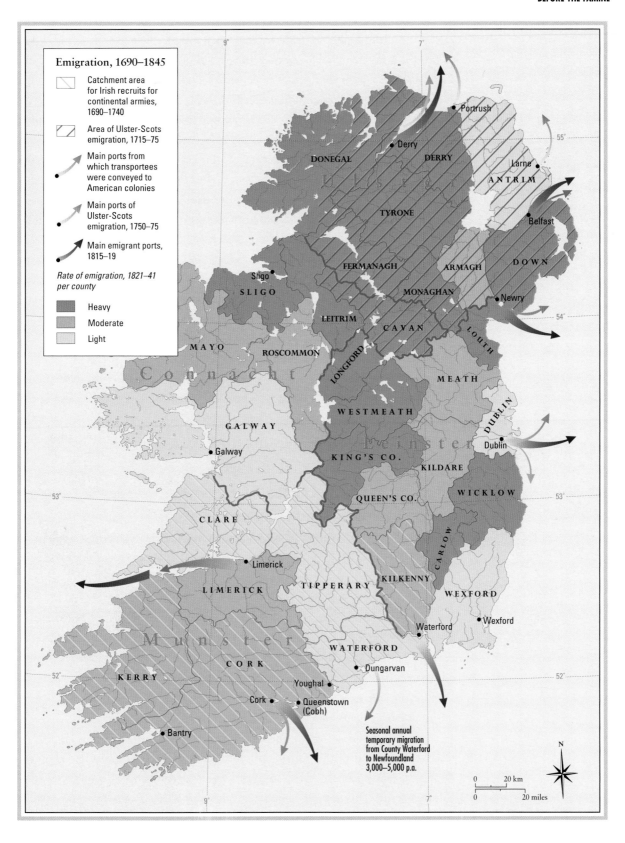

Emigration, 1690–1845

Catchment area for Irish recruits for continental armies, 1690–1740

Area of Ulster-Scots emigration, 1715–75

Main ports from which transportees were conveyed to American colonies

Main ports of Ulster-Scots emigration, 1750–75

Main emigrant ports, 1815–19

Rate of emigration, 1821–41 per county

Heavy

Moderate

Light

Portrush

Derry

DONEGAL

DERRY

Larne

ANTRIM

Belfast

TYRONE

Ulster

FERMANAGH

ARMAGH

DOWN

Sligo

MONAGHAN

Newry

SLIGO

LEITRIM

CAVAN

LOUTH

MAYO

ROSCOMMON

LONGFORD

MEATH

Connacht

WESTMEATH

GALWAY

Leinster

DUBLIN

Galway

KING'S CO.

Dublin

KILDARE

QUEEN'S CO.

WICKLOW

CLARE

CARLOW

LIMERICK

TIPPERARY

KILKENNY

WEXFORD

Limerick

Waterford

Wexford

Munster

WATERFORD

CORK

Dungarvan

KERRY

Youghal

Cork

Queenstown (Cobh)

Bantry

Seasonal annual temporary migration from County Waterford to Newfoundland 3,000–5,000 p.a.

N

0   20 km

0   20 miles

just over 8 million people, the only time such a figure has been achieved. Prior to this date, all estimates of population are no more than best guesses, lacking the statistical rigour of a modern census. That said, it is likely that prior to 1760, the total Irish population was less than 2.5 million.

The astonishing rise in the Irish population in the century before the Famine was remarked on by all contemporaries. It was accounted for by a number of factors: the widespread introduction of the easily cultivated and nutritious potato, which replaced grain as the staple diet of the poor; economic expansion, especially in agriculture, which raced ahead in the years of the Revolutionary Wars as Ireland helped to provision the British army; early marriages with high fertility rates; lower infant mortality; endless sub-division of tiny holdings.

The vast majority of Irish people were poor. However, this bald statement requires some qualification. There were considerable regional diversities. The rich limestone lands of the south and east supported a vigorous commercial agriculture in grain and cattle. Ireland remained a net exporter of food: it is estimated that about two million people in Britain were fed with produce imported from Ireland. In the first half of the 1840s, just before the Famine, there were about 5,000 livestock fairs held across the country each year. On the other hand, the poorer regions were wretched. In Connacht, the poorest province, 64 per cent of all farms were five acres or less. This was a subsistence economy with a vengeance. In one of the Connacht counties, Mayo, there were 475 people for each square mile of arable land. In general, the pattern of small holdings, rural overcrowding, severe poverty and lack of capital was more pronounced as one went further north and west.

The reliance on a single crop, the potato, had obvious risks in the event of crop failure or – the more common hazard – a smaller harvest than expected, which would mean some lean months in the coming year. The advantage of potatoes, however, was their exceptional nutritional value. The diet of the pre-Famine Irish poor, buttermilk and potatoes, was monotonous but healthy. Visitors commented with surprise on the physique of the Irish rural poor, comparing it favourably with that of their equivalents in richer countries. Other advantages included the ease with which potatoes could be cultivated – too easily, said the critics – and their ability to flourish on marginal land otherwise unsuitable for tillage.

There is no doubt that the potato monoculture in the poorer parts of Ireland discouraged the introduction of commercial agriculture. The few improving landlords who tried this met with fierce resistance. Commercial agriculture meant, among other things, the enclosure of land previously worked in common. The so-called rundale system of co-operative farming, in which long

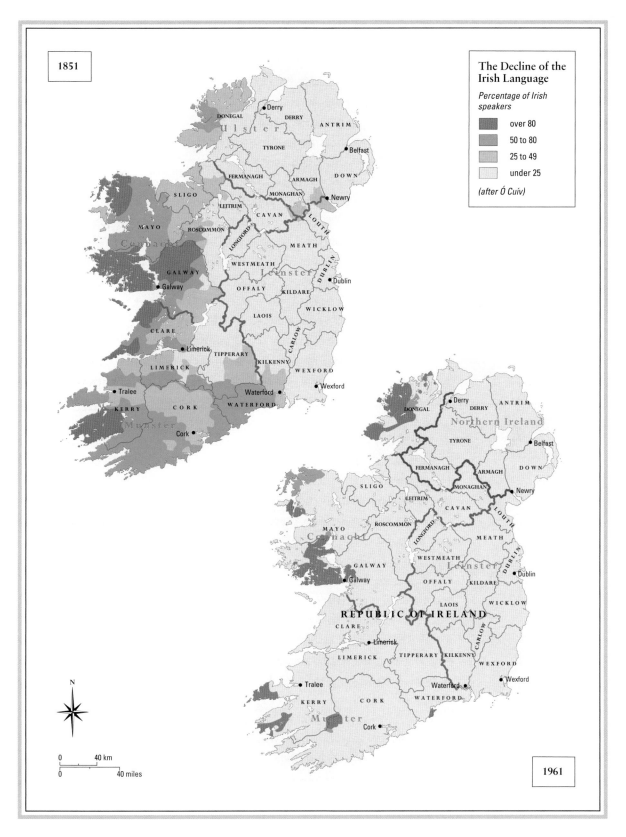

1851

The Decline of the
Irish Language

*Percentage of Irish
speakers*

over 80
50 to 80
25 to 49
under 25

(after Ó Cuív)

1961

N

0 ——— 40 km
0 ——— 40 miles

strips of land were farmed by extended families, was wonderfully fair in ensuring that no family member had a monopoly on the best land. Everyone got more or less the same share of good and bad land. This was socially cohesive and economically insane: it was a guarantee of low yields and offered no incentive to innovate or improve.

The great exception to this general picture was Ulster. Not only was reliance on the potato less than in the other three provinces, there was a thriving flax and linen industry in place since the late eighteenth century. Agriculture was more varied than elsewhere, and the domestic employment offered by linen weaving supplemented farm incomes. Moreover, the finishing and marketing of linen products was concentrated in Belfast, where it was the largest source of early industrial employment. Nor was Ulster exceptionalism something new. As early as the 1750s, John Wesley, the founder of Methodism, had reported that 'no sooner did we enter Ulster than we observed the difference. The ground was cultivated just as in England and the cottages not only neat but with doors, chimneys and windows.'

In the 1830s, the first stirrings of the Industrial Revolution were already visible in Belfast. The fact that industry roared ahead in Belfast and much of Ulster during the nineteenth century and failed to do so in the three southern provinces was one of the most significant developments in the story of modern Ireland.

In a changing world, no change is more fundamental than that of language. The death of languages is a melancholy feature of modernity: the standard speech of metropolitan elites overwhelms regional dialects and marginal languages. As modern states form themselves, the metropolitan language of commerce, law, administration and journalism exercises a powerful hold. An ambitious provincial, anxious to make a career in business, law or the civil service, must learn the language of power. The metropolitan explosion of newspapers and books in nineteenth-century Europe reinforced the tendency. In the twentieth century, radio, television and the internet accelerated it further. Regional speech – both patois and minority languages – suffered accordingly. Ireland has been no exception to this process.

English had obviously been the language of the Ascendancy in the eighteenth century. But the vast majority of the Irish population in 1800 spoke Irish, either as the sole vernacular or bilingually. By the mid 1830s, it was estimated that about 50 per cent of the population spoke the old language. The 1851 census gave a figure of 1.5 million people – less than a quarter of the whole – who spoke only Irish. This precipitate decline obviously reflects the devastating effects of the Famine. It was a decline that has continued unabated to the pres-

THE BIRTH OF "THE NATION"

ent day. The Famine merely accelerated a pre-existing pattern of decline.

Daniel O'Connell's first language had been Irish. As an adult, he was a champion of Catholic rights, the effective developer of what became the mainstream nationalist tradition, but he was indifferent to the Irish language to the point of hostility. He was able to mobilise mass opinion in Ireland first on a specifically Catholic issue and secondly on a national one – the demand for the repeal of the union – without ever touching on the cultural question of the decline of Irish. O'Connell effectively yoked Catholicism and nationalism together: the injection of language revival as a vital part of the nationalist project did not happen for another fifty years.

O'Connell's indifference to Irish was rooted in a utilitarian view of language itself. In 1833, admitting that the use of Irish was diminishing among the

John Blake Dillon, Thomas Davis and Charles Gavan Duffy, founders of The Nation *newspaper.*

Published 1828 by

College Green

A print of College Green in 1828 by Samuel F. Brocas.

J. Le Petit, 21, Grafton Str.ᵉ Dublin.

peasantry, he observed that 'the superior utility of the English tongue, as the medium of all modern communication, is so great, that I can witness without a sigh the gradual disuse of Irish'. This might be the voice of any ambitious provincial in Europe in the age before the idea of cultural nationalism established its dominance.

The anglicisation of Ireland is perhaps the key cultural development of the entire nineteenth century. Ironically, anglicisation marched hand-in-hand with nationalism. It was driven forward, as national movements tend to be, by an educated elite whose members were most likely to be anglophone. The Catholic middle class, which provided the officer corps of nationalism from O'Connell's time onward, moved in an explicitly anglophone world: it was no accident that the south-east of the island, that forcing house of modernity, was also the most anglicised part. Provincial newspapers, hugely influential in the spread of nationalist ideas, were published in English. The growing number of Catholic secondary fee-paying schools – aimed at the children of the middle class – increasingly modelled themselves on the English public schools. Education in the liberal professions, especially the law and medicine, was not just in English but closely adhered to English models. There was a great irony in all this: just as Ireland was moving farther from England politically, it was drawing closer to it culturally. By the mid-century, the immense prestige of an England approaching the apogee of her power – the workshop of the world, rich beyond the dreams of earlier generations – had a powerful gravitational pull for all within its orbit.

On 15 October 1842, the first edition of *The Nation* appeared in Dublin. The founders were Charles Gavan Duffy, a self-educated journalist; John Blake Dillon, a barrister; and Thomas Davis, barrister and minor poet. All were provincials from middle-class backgrounds: Dillon and Duffy were the sons of shopkeepers, Davis of an army surgeon.

The Nation was an astonishing success, at one point in the 1840s claiming a readership of almost 250,000. It was a radical nationalist paper. Although it supported O'Connell's repeal campaign, its emphasis was different to his. Where O'Connell was basically utilitarian in temperament, The Nation was Romantic. The Romantic movement had swept across Europe in the previous generation in reaction to the cool, calculating classicism of the Enlightenment. The surging music of Beethoven, the lyrical exuberance of Wordsworth and Byron, the sublime landscapes of Caspar David Friedrich: all were part of a common sensibility. This was what *The Nation* tapped into.

In political terms, Young Ireland – as the group clustered around *The Nation* became known – introduced a different strain of nationalist thought to Ireland. It was heavily influenced by German Romanticism as mediated through the work of the Scottish writer Thomas Carlyle. The nation was defined less in legal terms – popular sovereignty and the will of the people – than in cultural. It was literary – Davis was the pre-eminent popular poet of his day and some of his poems are still popular in ballad form – and it wished to promote a distinctively national literature. It was the first national movement to propose a revival of the Irish language. It emphasised the iconography of modern Irish nationalism: the harps and shamrocks, round towers and Irish wolfhounds, and introduced the tricolour flag. One of the Young Irelanders, Thomas Francis Meagher, brought the green, white and orange flag back from Paris in 1848, an obvious imitation of the revolutionary tricoleur.

Young Ireland was a repeal ginger group but relations between it and O'Connell were tense. In part, it represented a generational challenge to the elderly leader. But there was more than that. O'Connell's utilitarianism had led him to accept, however reluctantly, a confessional context for his campaigns. His was a substantially a Catholic movement. Young Ireland, with its emphasis on culture, proposed a more inclusive definition of nationality. It was rooted in different soil to the non-sectarianism of the United Irishmen in the 1790s but the fruits were very similar. O'Connell emphasised the practical politics of Catholic numbers, Young Ireland the idealist politics of a nation in which common citizenship would override religious differences.

In 1845, the British government established three universities in Ireland, the so-called Queen's Colleges, at Belfast, Cork and Galway. They were founded on a strictly non-sectarian basis. No state funding was provided for the support of chairs of theology, although private endowments were not forbidden. The campaign for a Catholic university had been a major demand from O'Connell and the hierarchy and the British hoped that the Queen's Colleges would satisfy the demand. Not so. O'Connell and the bishops denounced the 'godless colleges' and re-doubled their campaign for a specifically Catholic institution in which the church, not the state, would hold the reins.

Young Ireland welcomed the Queen's Colleges as a major step forward. They recoiled from a confessionalism that effectively coupled Irish identity with Catholicism. Davis himself was a Protestant. There was a terrible irony here: O'Connell's populism was democratic; Young Ireland's idealism was not. It was an elite subset of nationalism with shallow roots among the people, for all the popularity of *The Nation*.

This fault line in Irish nationalism would reappear. In the meantime, Davis died tragically young in 1845. O'Connell himself, his prestige reduced since the climb down at Clontarf and in ever declining health, would die in May 1847. And Ireland all unknowing stood on the brink of the greatest natural catastrophe in her history.

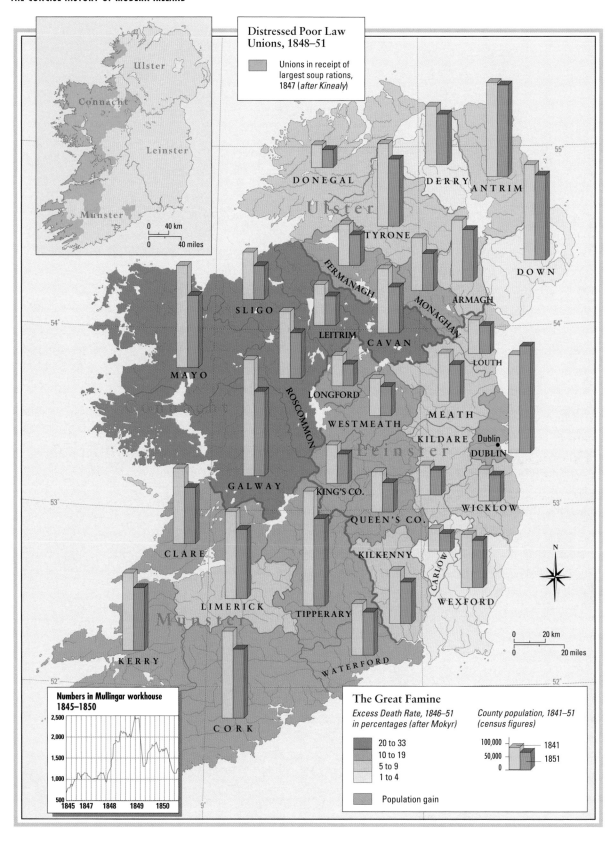

Distressed Poor Law
Unions, 1848–51

Unions in receipt of
largest soup rations,
1847 (*after Kinealy*)

Ulster

Connacht

Leinster

Munster

0   40 km

0   40 miles

DONEGAL

DERRY

ANTRIM

Ulster

TYRONE

FERMANAGH

MONAGHAN

ARMAGH

DOWN

SLIGO

LEITRIM

CAVAN

LOUTH

MAYO

LONGFORD

ROSCOMMON

WESTMEATH

MEATH

KILDARE   Dublin

DUBLIN

Leinster

GALWAY

KING'S CO.

WICKLOW

QUEEN'S CO.

CLARE

KILKENNY

CARLOW

LIMERICK

TIPPERARY

WEXFORD

Munster

KERRY

WATERFORD

N

CORK

0   20 km

0   20 miles

**Numbers in Mullingar workhouse
1845–1850**

2,500
2,000
1,500
1,000
500
1845   1847   1848   1849   1850

The Great Famine

*Excess Death Rate, 1846–51
in percentages (after Mokyr)*

20 to 33
10 to 19
5 to 9
1 to 4

Population gain

*County population, 1841–51
(census figures)*

100,000
50,000
0

1841
1851

CHAPTER 5

THE GREAT HUNGER

The Great Hunger 1845–52

In June 1845, a new and mysterious potato blight appeared for the first time in Europe, in Belgium. By September, it had made its way to Ireland. It resulted in the loss of about one-third of the Irish potato harvest that year. It was a crisis but not a disaster. The blight had appeared late in the year and much of the crop was already harvested when it struck. Even so, the failure of the staple crop on such a scale created a major social problem. It was not unprecedented. There had been partial failures of the crop in every decade of the nineteenth century. The difference was – although no one knew it at the time – that this was a new, virulent and utterly mysterious kind of blight.

The Tory government of Sir Robert Peel responded promptly. Peel had been chief secretary of Ireland from 1812 to 1818 and had provided £250,000 for the relief of distress during food shortages in 1817, in the course of which about 50,000 people had died. Although a Tory and a bitter opponent of O'Connell, he was a realist and it was he who finally introduced the legislation for the Catholic Emancipation act of 1829.

In November 1845, Peel's government spent £100,000 on buying and distributing Indian corn from the United States. It set up a commission to study the causes of the blight and instituted a series of public works which provided subsistence wages for the poor. Peel was a free trader but not an ideologue. Government assistance of this kind was contrary to the principles of free trade, which believed that the self-regulating internal logic of the economic system could only be distorted by government interference. None the less, Peel's government did intervene strongly and promptly in the face of such an urgent crisis.

In the summer of 1846, however, the Tory government fell. Ironically, its

In the period from 1300 to 1900 there were up to 30 severe famines in Ireland, about a dozen in the period 1290–1400 alone, and another dozen between 1500 and 1750. After 1750 there were several serious regional famines, culminating in the great national famine of 1845–49.

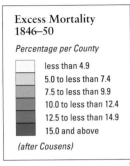

Excess Mortality 1846–50

Percentage per County

	less than 4.9
	5.0 to less than 7.4
	7.5 to less than 9.9
	10.0 to less than 12.4
	12.5 to less than 14.9
	15.0 and above

(after Cousens)

defeat came as a result of its own success in forcing through the repeal of the Corn Laws. These laws, the great symbolic target of all free traders for a generation, had placed restrictions on the importation of grain into the United Kingdom and had had the effect of acting as a kind of hidden subsidy to large landed interests.

The new Whig government was led by Lord John Russell. It was much more doctrinaire in its espousal of free trade principles and instinctively less likely than Peel had been to bend them or otherwise trim in the face of circumstance.

This had serious consequences in Ireland, for there was a wholesale failure of the potato crop in the summer of 1846. The blight reappeared earlier that year, before any harvesting could begin. This was the real beginning of the Great Famine.

The distress of the previous year had clearly left parts of the population in a poor position to cope with the shattering effects of total potato failure. The response of the Whig government in London was to reduce grain importation into Ireland and to attempt to run down public works schemes. Despite this, almost 500,000 desperate people were employed in such public works by the end of 1846 and nearly half as many again three months later. Contrary to its own instincts, the government established soup kitchens to feed the people in 1847. But its

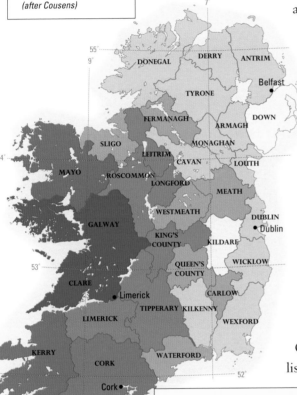

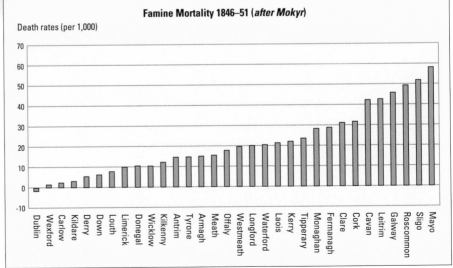

Famine Mortality 1846–51 (*after Mokyr*)

Death rates (per 1,000)

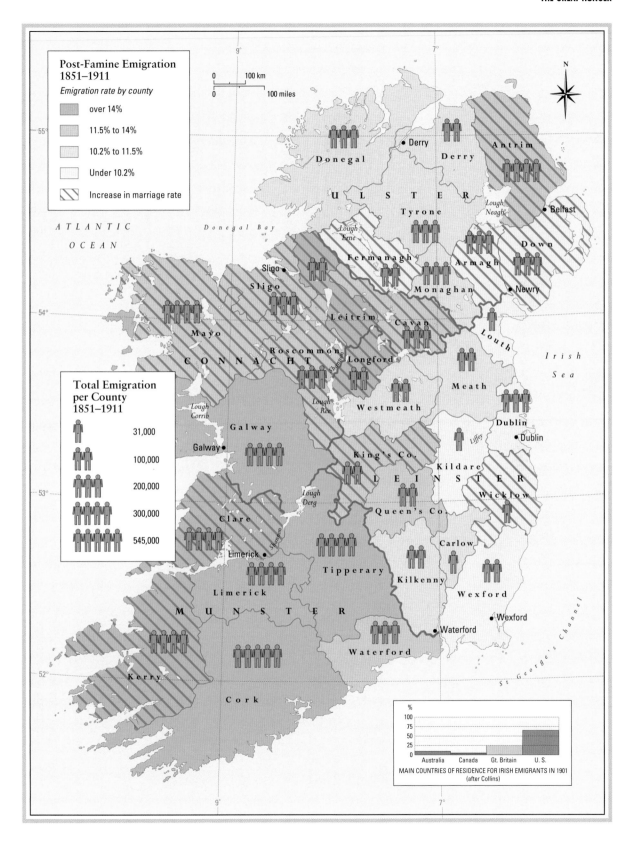

Post-Famine Emigration
1851–1911

Emigration rate by county

- over 14%
- 11.5% to 14%
- 10.2% to 11.5%
- Under 10.2%
- Increase in marriage rate

Total Emigration
per County
1851–1911

	31,000
	100,000
	200,000
	300,000
	545,000

MAIN COUNTRIES OF RESIDENCE FOR IRISH EMIGRANTS IN 1901
(after Collins)

Australia   Canada   Gt. Britain   U. S.

ATLANTIC OCEAN

Donegal Bay

Irish Sea

St George's Channel

ULSTER

CONNACHT

LEINSTER

MUNSTER

Donegal · Derry · Derry · Antrim · Belfast · Tyrone · Lough Neagh · Fermanagh · Lough Erne · Armagh · Down · Monaghan · Newry · Sligo · Leitrim · Cavan · Louth · Mayo · Roscommon · Longford · Westmeath · Meath · Lough Corrib · Lough Ree · Galway · Galway · King's Co. · Kildare · Dublin · Dublin · Lough Derg · Queen's Co. · Wicklow · Clare · Limerick · Tipperary · Carlow · Kilkenny · Wexford · Limerick · Waterford · Wexford · Waterford · Kerry · Cork

Shannon · Liffey

69

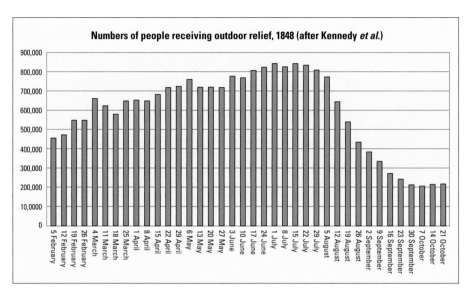

heart was not in it and they were closed down again at the end of that disastrous year.

Why did the government respond in such a cold-blooded way?

It was an article of faith in Westminster that Ireland was a social and economic mess. Its landlords were feckless and reactionary, not given to the sort of modernising improvements that had transformed English agriculture. The tenants were seen as a slothful human mass kept in a permanent state of backward subsistence by their reliance on the potato. The doctrinaire free traders wanted a wholesale shakeout of Irish agriculture: enclosure, modernisation, assisted passage schemes for tenants who were surplus to requirements, and so on. Because none of this was happening or likely to happen, Ireland was regarded by the free-trading Whigs as a chronic invalid.

In their eyes, the Famine was the inevitable consequence of this situation and an opportunity to remedy it. To many Whigs who were also devoutly evangelical Protestants, the Famine could be seen as the wrath of a righteous Providence.

The government's strategic aim was to minimise its own direct involvement in Famine relief and make Ireland responsible for bearing the cost. The cost of local relief was to be borne by Irish landlords; the Poor Law system was expected to be the means whereby relief was given. This strategy was grounded in an assertion that a local crisis should be treated locally and should not become a burden on national finances. This assertion dovetailed neatly with the core value of free trade, that government interference in the economic mechanism was harmful and damaging in itself. There was no doubt that free trade had made Britain rich. But now it was making Ireland starve.

After the failure of 1846, people were reduced to eating seed potatoes. Ironically, the crop did not fail in 1847 but yields were low because so little had

In the long term, the union of Great Britain and Ireland was a loser. The Famine fatally weakened the moral legitimacy of British rule in Ireland. In the eyes of Irish nationalists, the constitutional assertion that Ireland was a fully integrated part of the metropolitan British state seemed more and more a fiction. Britain treated Ireland not as an equal part of the United Kingdom but as a troublesome colony.

The Famine radicalised nationalists. It coincided with Europe's 'year of revolutions', 1848. Just as the United Irishmen of the 1790s had been inspired by the French Revolution of 1789, so now the radical Young Irelanders – John Mitchel, William Smith O'Brien and others – were inspired by the Paris revolution that established the second republic in February 1848. They and others had formed themselves into the Irish Confederation in 1847 on the occasion of their final break with the Repealers.

The movement was riddled with government informers and spies. Mitchel

LIG.

This illustration of the famine-stricken village of Tullig appeared in The Illustrated London News *on 15 December 1849, but by then the generosity of the British public had been blunted by repetition of the tragic conditions of the masses. Besides, Great Britain had itself suffered a severe economic recession in 1847, and its sympathy for Ireland's problems had waned following the return of 36 Irish MPs in the general election of that year committed to Repeal of the Act of Union. This smacked of ingratitude in the eyes of the British public, a view compounded by the Young Ireland rebellion of 1848.*

was arrested in May and convicted on a charge of treason-felony. He was transported for fourteen years, first in Bermuda and later in Van Diemen's Land (Tasmania). He escaped to America in 1853. There, he wrote *Jail Journal*, a bitterly anglophobe polemic that later became one of the sacred texts of Irish nationalism. He practiced journalism and supported the Confederacy in the American civil war.

The remaining Confederation leaders were effectively harried out of Dublin by government pressure. They tried to raise troops for a possible autumn rising in Tipperary and Kilkenny. They held a meeting at Ballingarry, Co. Tipperary in July 1848 to discuss the way forward. A majority was for avoiding armed action, at least for the moment. A minority, led by O'Brien, was in favour. The issue was forced by a company of police which entered the village and took up

The revolutionary movement popularly known as Fenianism originated in the hugely expanding Irish immigrant community in the USA, whose attention remained focused on Ireland as a result of their difficulties in integrating and the prejudice they experienced. While in theory a secret society it quickly attracted police attention when it put itself on a national footing, and its rising was a dismal failure, though the government's handling of it helped mobilise nationalist opinion in a way the Fenians themselves had never managed.

a position in the house of Mrs McCormack, a widow. Some of O'Brien's more enthusiastic supporters attacked this position. Two insurgents were killed before the arrival of police reinforcements brought the affray to an end.

It was derided as the battle of the Widow McCormack's cabbage patch. But it was also remembered as the rising of 1848. However inflated that claim might have been, it was typical of the Young Ireland achievement. They were propagandists rather than men of action. Their legacy was the creation of a myth – or at least a part of a myth. While mainstream nationalism would eventually revive itself along a broadly O'Connellite model – constitutional politics and the support of the church – the memory of '48, like that of '98, was a reminder of other possibilities. Young Ireland, like the United Irishmen, became part of an internal opposition within Irish nationalism.

The biggest winners of all in the fallout from the Famine were the wealthier tenants, although this was by no means obvious at the time. In the midst of the most appalling starvation and destitution, they maintained their social position. Not all tenants were poor. On the contrary, a comfortable tenant class and their merchant cousins in the towns survived the Famine very well. Once again, it is instructive to look at the foundation dates of Catholic institutions in order to appreciate how economically vigorous parts of the Catholic community remained in the Famine years. Kilkenny's Cathedral of the Assumption was begun in 1843; building continued until 1857. The parish church of St Mary's in Clonmel, Co. Tipperary, is dated to 1837–50. St Aidan's Cathedral, Enniscorthy, Co. Wexford (1843–8) was designed by Pugin, no less. He also designed the Loreto convent in nearby Gorey.

All these examples are within the rich south-eastern quadrant, where there were communities of Catholics wealthy enough to endow and erect such impressive structures at a time when the country was being engulfed in a demographic cataclysm. Nor was the process any longer the exclusive preserve of the south-east. The Catholic cathedral of St Patrick in Armagh was begun in 1840; the Franciscan church in Galway dates from 1849; the cathedral of SS Peter and Paul in Ennis, Co. Clare was consecrated in 1843; that of St Mary's in Killarney (Pugin again) in 1855 after thirteen years a-building.

While the real explosion in Catholic institutional building does not happen until the second half of the nineteenth century, what is significant is the degree to which the process is already well established before and during the Famine. The people who paid for all this – the Catholic provincial middle class – were the group that profited most from the Famine.

The landlords and the whole ascendancy world were weakened. The rural poor were decimated. The social engineering desired by the doctrinaire free traders was well under way. Farm sizes grew. Sub-division of holdings was ended. Enclosures proceeded and the system of communal agriculture was finally abandoned in the west in favour of individual holdings. Marriages were postponed until tenancies could be inherited; younger children had to shift for themselves, often by emigrating. There was a deeply unsentimental social calculus in post-Famine Ireland. Among tenants, the watchword was 'never again', even though (or perhaps because) theirs was the class that emerged least scathed from the Famine. In a sense, the dirty work that enabled them to become the dominant social force in Ireland from the 1880s on had been done for them. And it could all be blamed on the British.

The Catholics who did well out of the Famine were the backbone of the land movement, of Parnell's electorate, of the Catholic laity and clergy, of the Gaelic Athletic Association, and of all subsequent nationalist agitation. It was their class that was celebrated and sentimentalised in Charles Kickham's *Knocknagow* and other novels of the virtuous rural life. It was their grandchildren, by and large, who inherited the independent Irish state in 1922.

Population of Ireland 1841–1911	
1841	8,175,000
1851	6,552,000
1861	5,799,000
1871	5,412,000
1881	5,175,000
1891	4,705,000
1901	4,459,000
1911	4,390,000

The locations of churches and other buildings designed in whole or part by the prestigious father and son architects, A.W.N. Pugin and E.W. Pugin. These buildings testify to the wealth of the Catholic middle class in Victorian Ireland.

St. Aidan's Cathedral, Enniscorthy, Co. Wexford.

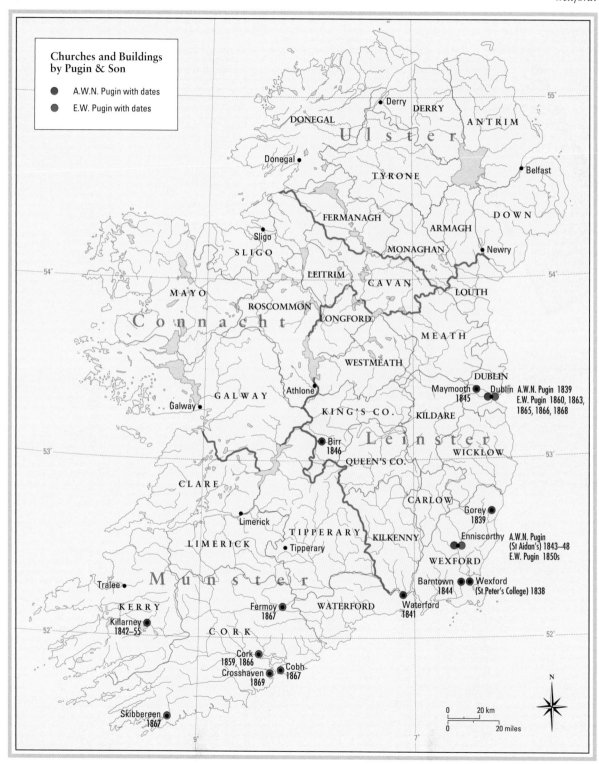

Churches and Buildings by Pugin & Son

● A.W.N. Pugin with dates
● E.W. Pugin with dates

Derry

DERRY

DONEGAL

ANTRIM

U l s t e r

Donegal

Belfast

TYRONE

D O W N

FERMANAGH

ARMAGH

Sligo

MONAGHAN

Newry

S L I G O

LEITRIM

C A V A N

LOUTH

M A Y O

ROSCOMMON

LONGFORD

C o n n a c h t

M E A T H

WESTMEATH

DUBLIN

Maymooth 1845

Dublin

A.W.N. Pugin 1839
E.W. Pugin 1860, 1863, 1865, 1866, 1868

Athlone

GALWAY

KING'S CO.

KILDARE

Galway

L e i n s t e r

Birr 1846

WICKLOW

QUEEN'S CO.

CLARE

CARLOW

Gorey 1839

Limerick

TIPPERARY

KILKENNY

Enniscorthy

A.W.N. Pugin (St Aidan's) 1843–48
E.W. Pugin 1850s

LIMERICK

Tipperary

WEXFORD

Barntown 1844

Wexford
(St Peter's College) 1838

Tralee

M u n s t e r

Waterford 1841

KERRY

Fermoy 1867

WATERFORD

Killarney 1842–55

C O R K

Cork 1859, 1866

Cobh 1867

Crosshaven 1869

Skibbereen 1867

N

0   20 km

0   20 miles

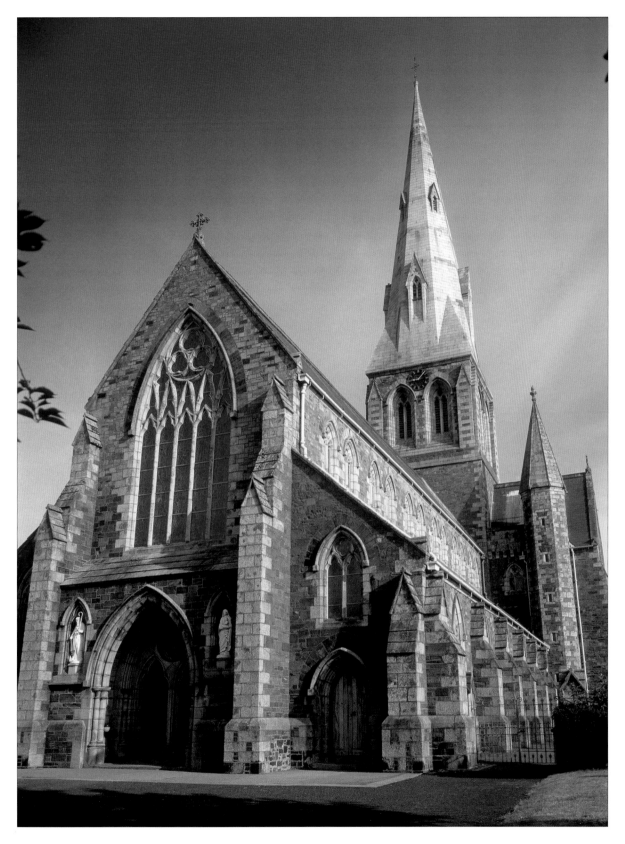

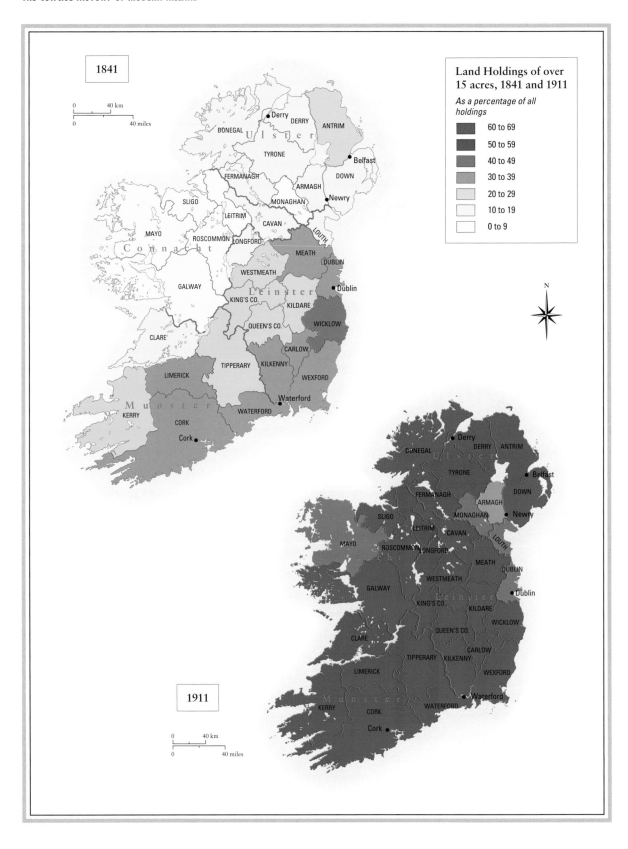

CHAPTER 6

AFTER THE FAMINE
Land, Fenians and the Industrial
Revolution in Ulster 1852–68

The Famine changed Ireland irrevocably. It ushered in the age of the farmer. Farmers became the key social group in post-Famine Ireland. First as tenants, later as owner-occupiers, their material interests became associated with those of the nation itself, a situation that persisted until the economic changes of the 1960s shifted the balance of power towards the urban middle class.

The land question was the key question in post-Famine. In time, land and the national question became one. In their own eyes, farmers were the real Irish nation. Agriculture was simply the most important economic activity in the country and much of the economic life of provincial Ireland depended on the prosperity of farmers. In the towns, industries such as brewing and distilling drew their raw materials from the countryside.

As farm sizes increased, the basic shape of modern Irish agriculture emerged. The key change was the shift from tillage to pasture. A great deal of the tillage economy of the pre-Famine period had been of the subsistence kind. That ended, as almost all Irish agriculture went on to a commercial footing. Large farms emerged, particularly in those flat eastern counties near Dublin which were best suited for pasture. These holdings, often referred to as 'ranches', were to be the source of ongoing resentment from smallholders. In part, this was due to the no-nonsense commercialism of the ranchers.

The ranchers were an interesting group. Many were Catholics and nationalists, shopkeepers and other town dwellers who had accumulated some capital and were in a position either to rent or buy the large holdings for grazing. There was huge social prestige attached to the ownership or control of land. The ranchers were a new rural elite. Their position within the broader nationalist consensus was anomalous. On the one hand, they often provided the kind of social leadership and financial support on which nationalist movements depended; on the other, they drew the fire of smallholders who asserted the superiority of tillage as the backbone of self-sufficient family farms. There was a plenty of potential in all this for class war in the countryside – and it did break out from time to time, with cattle drives and other actions directed against the ranchers – but in general it was kept under control. Unity in the nationalist community overbore every other consideration, especially until the hated landlord system was dismantled in the early twentieth century.

Post-Famine Ireland was never classless. On the contrary, small social differences were often keenly felt in a manner typical of a provincial small-town and rural society. Both the rural and urban working classes – the landless agricultural labourers and the unskilled slum dwellers in the cities – were held in something between disdain and contempt by the prevailing petit bourgeois culture. Yet the imperative demands of national solidarity never permitted the development of fully blown class politics.

In the aftermath of the Famine, nationalist Ireland was exhausted and demoralised. As politics atrophied, the Catholic Church filled the void. It was a church which was reinventing itself. The pre-Famine church had had a broadly Gallican thrust. This meant an emphasis on the autonomy of local bishops in matters of a civil and temporal nature. Spiritual matters were, of course, subject to full papal authority. Gallican ideas contrasted with ultramontanism, the view which stressed the central authority of Rome in all matters affecting Catholics.

In 1850, Paul Cullen was appointed archbishop of Armagh. Three years later, he was translated to Dublin and in 1866 he became the first Irish cardinal. He had been born in Co. Kildare in 1803 and ordained in Rome in 1829. In 1832, he was appointed rector of the Irish college in Rome. His entire formation as a cleric had therefore taken place in the shadow of the Vatican. He was recognised from the first as a person of exceptional ability: hard-working, rigorous, disciplined and intellectually accomplished. Cullen was an ultramontane by conviction and temperament alike.

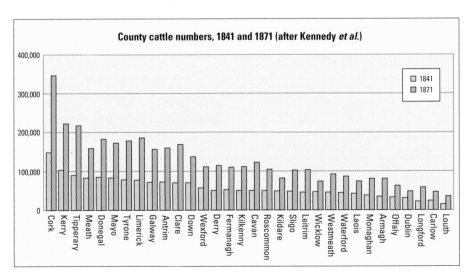

County cattle numbers, 1841 and 1871 (after Kennedy *et al.*)

He was Rome's man in Ireland and he left an imprint on the Irish Church that was not seriously shaken until the clerical sex scandals of the 1990s. The Catholic Church became the undisputed centre of moral authority in nationalist Ireland. No politician could ignore it.

The process of weakening the Gallican element began with the first major initiative of Cullen's episcopacy. In 1850, on instructions from Rome, he summoned a national synod of the church at Thurles, Co. Tipperary. It was the first Irish national synod since the twelfth century and the first formal meeting of all the bishops of Ireland since the seventeenth. The synod predictably redoubled the church's condemnation of the 'godless colleges' and resolved on the establishment of a Catholic university. It also adopted decrees designed to tighten discipline in the Irish church; to ensure that matters in dispute were referred to Rome for decision, thus weakening discretionary power at diocesan level; and to introduce sodalities and devotions for the laity uniformly throughout the country. The whole thrust of the Synod of Thurles was to centralise and standardise as far as possible and to introduce 'Roman' practices at the expense of traditional forms of local piety, many of which the ultramontanes regarded as little better than superstition.

Much has been made of the so-called devotional revolution in the Irish church. This was the process whereby Catholicism progressively abandoned traditional folk practices: patterns (gatherings at traditional shrines); wakes; stations (masses celebrated in private houses). The new emphasis was to be on uniform devotions conducted under formal clerical supervision in churches. Strict Sunday observance; regular attendance at confession and communion as decreed in canon law; the widespread introduction of continental devotions such as those to the Sacred Heart and later to the Immaculate Conception; benedictions; processions carefully marshalled and disciplined by the clergy;

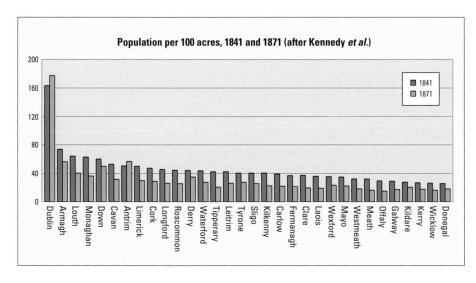

Population per 100 acres, 1841 and 1871 (after Kennedy *et al.*)

sodalities, confraternities; public retreats and missions: all these features were characteristic of the devotional revolution. Some were already in place before Cullen's time, but he gave them all his enthusiastic and urgent support, quickening the pace of change.

As with politics, the devotional revolution was most developed in the southeast of the island, less so (until Cullen's time) as one went north and west. The growth of church building in the second half of the century, and the assertive and dominating presence of so many fine churches, reflected the new centrality of the parish church in the lives of the faithful. In a sense, it represented the industrialisation of Irish Catholicism. The churches were like spiritual factories, where people now had to travel to worship at set times and in a disciplined manner ordained by their clerical overseers.

After the failure of 1848, the remaining Young Irelanders scattered. Some, like John Mitchel, were transported. Others, like John Blake Dillon, escaped abroad before taking advantage of an amnesty in 1855 to return without ever again being a major force in politics. Charles Gavan Duffy was a Westminster MP for three years but gave it up in disgust and emigrated to Australia. He lived a long life, became prime minister of Victoria in 1871 and accepted a knighthood two years later before ending his days in retirement in the south of France.

The source of Gavan Duffy's disgust was an abortive attempt to organise Irish nationalists at Westminster. It started in the wake of the Famine, when two organisations were established – one on Ulster, the other in Leinster – to secure the rights of tenants at a time when they were under increasing threat of eviction from landlords. In the three southern provinces, tenants had neither customary nor statutory protection from their landlords' whims. However, the so-called Ulster Custom obtained in most of the north. It was never universal either in application or definition, but essentially it meant that a departing tenant could dispose of his tenancy to the highest bidder, subject to the landlord's approval of the newcomer. It usually included compensation to the value of any improvements that the departing tenant had made.

The Ulster Tenant Right Association was established in 1847, mainly to protect Presbyterian tenants from Anglican landlords. It aimed to make the Ulster Custom (free sale, as it called it) statutory. In a remarkable development, the Ulster and Leinster associations merged in 1850 to form the Irish Tenant League, a genuinely non-sectarian and national association. By now the Ulster Custom had become more elastically defined, which definition formed the so-called Three Fs – free sale, fair rent (to be set by an independent tribunal) and fixity of tenure (no eviction if rents properly paid). The Three Fs became the core demand of all agrarian tenant groups for the next generation.

The glad, confident morning of the Irish Tenant League did not last long. It took little to detach the Catholic south from the Protestant north. The revival of the Catholic Church in Britain had led to an attempt to restore the old pre-Reformation dioceses. This provoked a Protestant reaction and the government rushed through legislation forbidding the Catholics from using any of the traditional territorial names for their restored dioceses: these name were retained exclusively for the Established Church. Irish Liberal MPs, most of them supporters of the Irish Tenant League but also dependent on Catholic votes, formed an Independent Irish Party in protest against the legislation. Ignoring Gavan Duffy's advice to have nothing to do with the new party, the Tenant League threw its support behind it. In the 1852 election, 48 MPs were returned in the party's interest, all of them pledged to independent opposition. Significantly, however, not one of them was from Ulster: the overt association between the party and a Catholic agitation was simply too rich for the Protestant blood. The so-called 'League of North and South' may have been a chimera, but it had been a benign one. There was never to be another one.

The party itself was a fiasco. Known variously as the Irish Brigade and the Pope's Brass Band, it was completely compromised when two of its leading figures, William Keogh and John Sadleir, accepted government office in defiance of their election pledges. Moreover, it made the serious error of picking a quarrel with the Catholic Church in the person of Cullen, not a man to be crossed. Sadleir came to a bad end: a director of the Tipperary Joint-Stock Bank, he was £200,000 overdrawn on his own account when he committed suicide in London, whereupon the bank was discovered to be insolvent. Depositors lost almost £400,000. Keogh, after a career as a notably reactionary judge, eventually died by his own hand as well.

It was these squalid transactions that drove Gavan Duffy into despairing exile. But the buffoonery of the Pope's Brass Band gave parliamentary politics generally a bad name. It all seemed a leaden age after the heroics of O'Connell and the cataclysm of the Famine. Gavan Duffy was not alone in feeling a sense of disgust. It was shared by many, especially by others who had been involved in Young Ireland. And some of them had an alternative.

No sub-set of Young Ireland was of greater importance for the future than the Fenians. The Fenian Brotherhood or Irish Republican Brotherhood (IRB) was founded jointly in Dublin and New York in 1858. The Dublin founder was James Stephens, an 1848 veteran who had fled to Paris where he had involved himself in various revolutionary secret societies. From them, he acquired the organisational principles he put in place in Ireland. The basic Fenian structure was this: a local leader, known as a centre, was chosen. Each centre chose nine captains who chose nine sergeants who chose nine men. Information was passed to each rank on a need-to-know basis only. Within a few years, Stephens had tramped the country and established a national network based on this structure.

The New York organisation was principally the work of John O'Mahony, another 1848 veteran. The introduction of Irish-America into the equation was a critical development: no subsequent nationalist movement has been indifferent to the enormous potential of the transatlantic disapora.

The Fenians believed in the force of arms. They were a secret, militant, revolutionary society dedicated to the violent overthrow of British rule in Ireland and the establishment in its place of an independent Irish republic. They were uninterested in politics, with its trimming and prevarication. They borrowed their methods from the European left-wing secret society tradition. Which brought them head to head with the Catholic Church.

The ultramontane Catholicism of Pope Pius IX was bitterly opposed to revolutionary secret societies. The church had been an uncompromising enemy of revolutionary France and a strong supporter of the reactionary regimes established after the final defeat of Napoleon. These regimes had been overturned in 1848 and Pius himself had had to flee from Rome for two years.

In these circumstances, it was inevitable that the church in Ireland would regard the Fenians as part of an international conspiracy against the legitimate order. Cullen was no friend of the British state but he was determined to ensure that Irish opposition to it was firmly under church control. He exercised effective control over loose alliances of Irish MPs at Westminster in the 1850s and '60s, but these groups were never effective and never caught the public imagination.

The Fenians did. Stephens was a talented organiser and numbers swelled. In particular, Fenianism appealed to lower middle-class young men in the towns. This was a group significantly lower on the social scale than most of the Young Irelanders had been. In this sense, Fenianism played its own part in the democratisation of Irish nationalism.

Success inevitably meant police penetration, despite the cell structure. In 1865, Stephens and the leadership of the Fenians were arrested in a pre-emptive strike by the government. They had indeed been planning for a rising that year, hoping to exploit the services of Irish-American soldiers demobilised at the end of the American Civil War. The loss of momentum in 1865 was fatal and that generation of Fenians never recovered from it. Stephens dithered on his release from prison. He sailed to New York and became fatally embroiled in the poisonous internal politics of the Irish-Americans. Stephens was eventually deposed and a small group of American Fenians sailed to Ireland. In March

1867, they tripped off a feeble rising that was hardly more heroic as a feat of arms than 1848. But the aftermath was significant. First, the 1867 rising entered the apostolic succession of Irish rebellions. Second, Fenian prisoners became a focus of political agitation. Third, two of these prisoners were the subject of a rescue bid. A police van in Manchester containing the two Irish prisoners was attacked and the men released but a policeman was killed in the process. Three men, William Allen, Michael Larkin and William O'Brien, were hanged for this deed. These were the 'Manchester Martyrs' and their executions galvanised nationalist Ireland. The song 'God Save Ireland' was written in their memory and became the unofficial national anthem for the next two generations.

There was another kind of revolution in Ireland at the mid-nineteenth century. The Industrial Revolution hardly affected the three southern provinces but it transformed Ulster. The term itself refers to a complex series of economic advances that began in Britain from the 1780s onwards and spread gradually and unevenly through Western Europe in the nineteenth century. The key developments were the harnessing of steam power, the accelerated development

'Steerage emigrants', a wood engraving by Arthur Boyd Houghton, published in the Graphic, *March 1869, shows poor emigrants sailing the cheap steerage passage to North America.*

Shipyard workers at the turn of the century, Belfast.

of coal and iron mining, the move from domestic piece work by individual craftsmen to factory production by armies of semi-skilled and unskilled workers. This development meant the growth of industrial cities and a surge of population from the countryside to the towns.

The Industrial Revolution had originated in Britain, where it was mainly focused in the midlands, north and west. Ireland, with its lack of iron and coal, seemed unpromising territory. But the exception proved to be in eastern Ulster, where the centralisation of the linen bleaching industry in Belfast marked the first stage in the industrialisation of the province and the beginning of Belfast's phenomenal nineteenth-century expansion. Its population in 1808 was about 25,000; in 1901, it was almost 350,000.

In 1828, the York Street linen mill was established. An enormous premises by the industrial standards of the times, it became the focus of Belfast's pre-eminence as a centre of the international linen trade. By 1850, there were sixty-two such mills in Belfast alone. The need to import coal and flax – because the industry had expanded beyond the ability of local resources to supply the mills – meant the development of Belfast port. From this, there grew the shipbuilding industry which was the city's pride in the late Victorian and Edwardian eras.

In 1858 Edward Harland bought a small shipyard in Belfast Lough. Three years later, he went into partnership with Gustav Wilhelm Wolff. Harland & Wolff was to become one of the giants of British shipbuilding: it built the most famous ship ever to sail and sink, the *Titanic*, in 1912. A smaller yard, that of Workman Clark ('the wee yard'), was established on the Lagan in 1880 where it flourished until the Great War before finally closing in 1935.

It was not just linen and ships. The Belfast region produced other textiles, tobacco products, engineering and other commodities typical of the new industrial age. In effect, east Ulster became part of the economy of north-west Britain. Its economic fortunes could hardly have made a greater contrast with the agricultural provinces to the south, reeling from the effects of the Famine. The leaders of industry in Ulster were almost all Protestants: their identification with their co-religionists in Britain was augmented by common economic and material interests. Ulster was becoming more different, not less.

Behind the impressive modernity of industrial Ulster, however, there loomed *Belfast riots, 1886.*

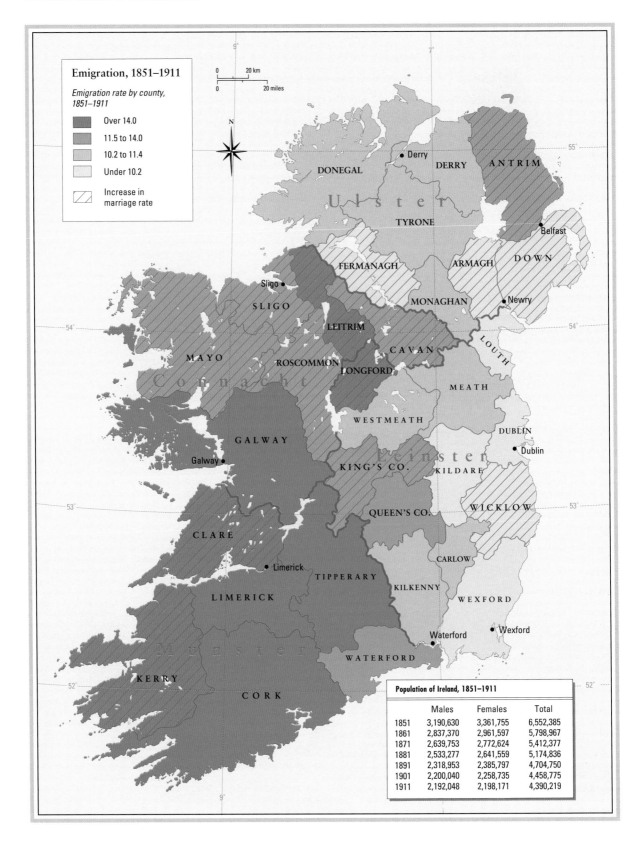

Emigration, 1851–1911

Emigration rate by county,
1851–1911

- Over 14.0
- 11.5 to 14.0
- 10.2 to 11.4
- Under 10.2
- Increase in marriage rate

Population of Ireland, 1851–1911			
	Males	Females	Total
1851	3,190,630	3,361,755	6,552,385
1861	2,837,370	2,961,597	5,798,967
1871	2,639,753	2,772,624	5,412,377
1881	2,533,277	2,641,559	5,174,836
1891	2,318,953	2,385,797	4,704,750
1901	2,200,040	2,258,735	4,458,775
1911	2,192,048	2,198,171	4,390,219

the long shadow of sectarian hatred. Industrialisation meant migration from country to town and the migrants brought their ancient enmities with them. As early as 1850, Belfast in particular was a city segregated by confessional allegiance, especially in working-class areas. There were serious inter-communal riots through the second half of the nineteenth century, a tradition that deepened in the twentieth and is still virulently present in the city today.

The nineteenth century was an age of faith. Religion was central to life and to people's belief systems in a way that is almost beyond the understanding of even the most devout modern believer. Religious differences were sharply felt, doctrinal and theological rivalries keenly contested. This was true of Europe in general. In Ireland, such differences were sharpened by the overlay of inherited ethnic and class polarities. But Ulster was a special case. Nowhere else in Ireland was the balance of populations so volatile and unstable or the burden of the past so oppressive. Ulster was not only running in a course different to that of the other three provinces. It was doing so in the face of internal divisions that had their roots in the seventeenth century and that were being renewed and strengthened in every generation.

There were severe riots in Belfast in 1857, 1864, 1872 and 1886, the latter in response to the threat of the first Home Rule bill. More people died in these disturbances than in Robert Emmet's rising, the rising of 1848 and the Fenian rising of 1867 combined, although you might sometimes be forgiven for thinking otherwise. The pattern was clear. Catholics from the countryside, come to work in the shipyards and mills, clustered together among their co-religionists in recognisable enclaves. Likewise, the Protestant poor liked to stay with their own kind. Inevitably, the interfaces between the two confessions were potential – and at regular intervals, actual – flashpoints.

Until the Industrial Revolution, Belfast had been an overwhelmingly Presbyterian town and one of a generally liberal temper. The inundation of the new proletariat changed that. But it was not the only force working for change. A critical transformation had occurred in Ulster Presbyterianism itself. A theological dispute between two parties within the church – dubbed Old Light and New Light – grew ever more intense in the first half of the nineteenth century. In general, New Light had dominated the church in the eighteenth century and had been associated with the liberalism that had found political expression in Presbyterian support for the United Irishmen. From 1800 on, however, the Old Light tendency renewed itself. It stressed a more traditional, inflexible Calvinism: inevitably, this entailed a less accommodating attitude towards Catholicism. The Old Light finally triumphed by 1840, marginalising its opponents. In that year, it established the General Assembly of the Presbyterian Church in Ireland – still the governing body of the church – along orthodox and traditional lines.

Heuston Station, Dublin, formerly Kingsbridge. It dates from 1844 and was built as the magnificent terminus for the Great Southern & Western Railway.

This conservative Presbyterianism got a further shot in the arm in 1859 during the dramatic events known as the Ulster Revival. This was an outbreak of populist piety or religious hysteria – take your pick according to preference – in eastern Ulster. It affected all Protestant denominations. As with all such manifestations, it emphasised conversion, personal re-birth and salvation, visions and every form of irrational excess.

At a time when Irish Catholicism was renewing itself dramatically under Cullen – emphasising those doctrines and devotional practices that were most remote from Protestantism – the Protestant churches, and especially the Presbyterians of Ulster, were engaged in an equal and opposite exercise. The churches, and their congregations, were moving further apart.

The intellectual leader of Old Light Presbyterianism was Rev. Henry Cooke, a trenchant opponent of O'Connell and Repeal. On the only occasion on which O'Connell ever visited Belfast – a significant fact in itself – Cooke challenged

him to a debate, which O'Connell uncharacteristically refused. Cooke laid much of the groundwork for the later unanimity of support among Ulster Protestants for the Union. His co-religionist Rev. Hugh Hanna, known as 'Roaring Hanna' because of his incendiary anti-Catholic street preaching, did nothing to dampen sectarian tensions, nor did Rev. Thomas Drew, whose sermon to Orangemen on 12 July 1857 referred *inter alia* to 'the arrogant pretenses of Popes and the outrageous dogmata of their blood-stained religion'. This was the prelude to ten days of sectarian rioting in which the Orangemen were enthusiastically assisted by the Belfast police.

It is not just an exercise in even-handedness to point out that Catholics could be just as absolutist in their claims as Protestants. The famous Dominican preacher, Fr Tom Burke – who had delivered the panegyric at the dedication the O'Connell monument in Glasnevin Cemetery, Dublin in 1869 – put things very bluntly in addressing an American audience three years later: "Take an Irishman, wherever he is found, all over the earth, and any casual observer will at once come to the conclusion, 'Oh he is an Irishman, he is a Catholic'. The two go together."

Burke's confident assertion was in no sense unrepresentative, nor was Burke himself a foaming incendiary, although not one to avoid religious controversy. He was a former Rector of the Irish College in Rome and a theological advisor to the Irish bishops at the Vatican Council of 1869–70. The point was that Catholics and Protestants lived in parallel mental and imaginative worlds. The universalism of one inevitably excluded the other, making 'the other side' ever more invisible and, in times of controversy or stress, less human.

Just as Catholicism and Protestantism increasingly emphasised their differences and asserted their particularities with growing vehemence, so their concomitant political demands were stated ever more shrilly. Asserting the virtues

*William Dargan
constructed the first
railway line in Ireland,
between Dublin and
Kingstown in 1831.*

of the tribe was now the order of the day. In the three southern provinces, with its overwhelmingly Catholic population, this prepared the way for enormous political and agrarian reforms. But in the Ulster cockpit, with its unstable sectarian geography, it was lethal.

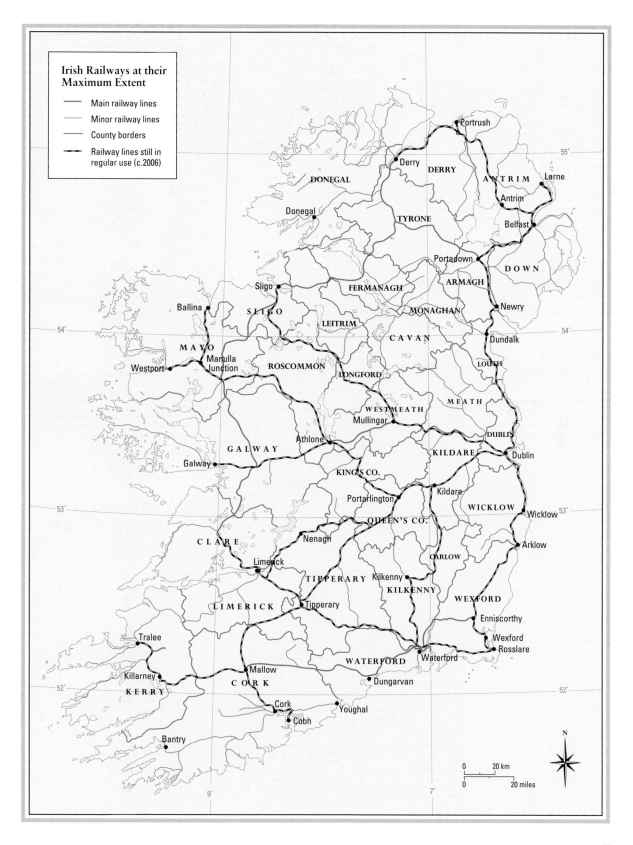

Irish Railways at their Maximum Extent

— Main railway lines
— Minor railway lines
— County borders
▬ Railway lines still in regular use (c.2006)

The Boyne Viaduct at Drogheda on the Dublin–Belfast line. Built in the 1850s, this photograph dates from about 1900.

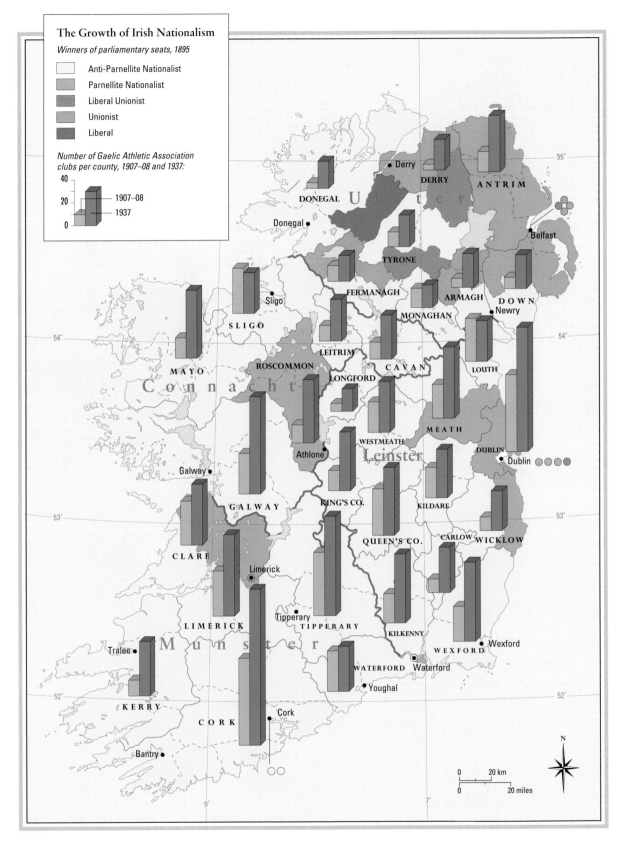

The Growth of Irish Nationalism

Winners of parliamentary seats, 1895

- Anti-Parnellite Nationalist
- Parnellite Nationalist
- Liberal Unionist
- Unionist
- Liberal

Number of Gaelic Athletic Association clubs per county, 1907–08 and 1937:

40
20
0
1907–08
1937

CHAPTER 7

UNCROWNED KING
Parnell and the New Nationalism
1869–91

The Clerkenwell bomb was the last and most dramatic action of the Fenian campaign. A leading Irish-American Fenian, Ricard O'Sullivan Burke, was arrested in London in November 1867. Burke was the Fenians' principal arms agent in Britain. He had been involved in the rising in Ireland earlier in the year and had been the main organiser of the Manchester prison van rescue that had resulted in the execution of the Manchester Martyrs. He had been betrayed by an informer. He was charged with treason-felony and lodged in Clerkenwell House of Detention in London.

His fellow-Fenians were determined to spring him. On the afternoon of Friday 13 December, a barrel of dynamite was placed against the wall of the prison. When it exploded, it demolished a sixty-foot section of the wall together with all the houses on the opposite

side of the street. Clerkenwell was a densely packed working-class area. Seventeen people died; one woman went mad; forty women gave birth prematurely. At least 120 were badly injured. And it was all for nothing. The plan had been betrayed to the prison authorities. Burke was in a double-locked cell and the exercise yard, where he was to have been, was deserted.

The destruction of life and property on such a scale shocked and outraged British public opinion. The new prime minister, William Ewart Gladstone, reacted more thoughtfully: he began to cast around for a series of reforms that would bind Ireland more closely to the British state by addressing legitimate grievances.

Gladstone's first legislative measure was the disestablishment of the Church of Ireland. Although the largest Protestant denomination in the country, it still accounted for barely 12 per cent of the total population. It had been the established church since Henry VIII's break with Rome in the 1530s and its position as the official state church had been confirmed by the Act of Union, which united it to the Church of England. Disestablishment therefore unravelled a key provision

Charles Stewart Parnell entered parliament in 1875 and was active in the 'obstructionist' faction of the Home Rule Party. Their intention was to obstruct the day-to-day business of parliament in order to highlight Irish issues.

THE GRAND OLD MAGICIAN'S IRISH POLICY

of the union settlement. The logic of this was not lost on unionists, for if one provision could be set aside what was to stop the whole thing being subverted?

Gladstone next turned to tackle an issue that went to the very heart of Irish discontent: land. In the aftermath of the Famine, the government had been obliged to pass a series of Encumbered Estates Acts, to provide a legal mechanism whereby debt-ridden estates could be sold off free of encumbrances. The effect was not just to transfer land from bankrupt to solvent landlords but to introduce the idea that the road to solving the Irish land problem ran through Westminster.

Before the Famine, relations between landlord and tenant was regarded as a simple matter of contract law, an agreement between two contracting parties. The relative strengths of the parties were deemed irrelevant. Government interference through legislation in what was regarded a free transaction between individuals was thought unnecessary and oppressive. The Encumbered Estates Acts changed all that. Parliament was now a player, since the law of contract had proved unequal to the task.

There were to be eighteen Irish land acts passed between 1870 and 1903, all intended to equalise the relationship between landlord and tenant by positive discrimination in favour of the latter. Gladstone's act of 1870 was the start of this process. It gave legal force to certain customary practices, in particular the Ulster Custom. A departing tenant now had the right to be compensated for improvements made by him and also to sell his interest to the highest bidder subject to the landlord's approval of the purchaser. These customary rights, which had been generally confined to the northern province, were now extended to the whole country by force of law.

On 1 September 1870 the Home Government Association was launched in Dublin by Isaac Butt, a barrister and former MP. Its basic demand was for some form of devolved autonomy for Ireland or, in the brilliantly vague term in which it couched the demand, home rule.

The term was deliberately elastic. In the early days, in Butt's formulation, it amounted to a call for devolved domestic parliaments for Ireland, Scotland and England (but not for Wales). Westminster would remain sovereign and would deal with foreign and imperial matters.

Part of home rule's early appeal lay with some members of the Church of Ireland who felt betrayed by disestablishment and who thought that a Dublin parliament could be a better safeguard for Protestant interests. Butt himself was a Protestant.

As the 1870s wore on, the home rule movement took on a more overtly nationalist hue. Constitutional nationalists and ex-Fenians were drawn to it; it also attracted the support of parish clergy, although not yet of the hierarchy. In

Opposite: *A complex character, the British Prime Minister William Ewart Gladstone (1809–98) developed an interest in Ireland for a number of reasons: one was a sense of moral responsibility, another a genuine belief that Ireland was a separate nation which needed distinct treatment, and a third a conviction that the preservation of the United Kingdom depended on constitutional reform.*

the 1874 general election that ousted Gladstone and installed Disraeli, candidates pledged to home rule won 59 seats. But they did not constitute a party in any modern sense. Butt was a gentlemanly but ineffective leader; he lost the support of many of his original Protestant adherents without gaining the confidence of the Catholic hierarchy; and the Fenian and neo-Fenian element among his MPs were effectively out of his control. From 1876 on, they began disruptive filibustering tactics in Westminster.

This unseemly challenge to the decorum of the house eventually forced a change in its rule with the introduction of the 'guillotine' to foreclose debates. It also threw up an alternative to Butt. His name was Charles Stewart Parnell. He was from an old Co. Wicklow landed family and was MP for Co. Meath since 1875. He ousted Butt as party leader in 1880.

The previous year, he had acquired an even more important position when he became president of the Land League. This organisation had been founded in October 1879 mainly due to the energy and drive of Michael Davitt, the son of an evicted tenant farmer from Co. Mayo. An ex-Fenian with a conviction for gun-running, Davitt was dedicated to the wholesale overthrow of the landlord system.

The founding of the Land League coincided with an agricultural depression and a consequent reduction in agricultural earnings. The threat of eviction loomed for tenants unable to pay their rent. Memories of the Famine only a generation old stiffened the determination to resist. Irish-American money provided the means to organise. A loose administrative structure meant that the best organised and most ruthless could dominate the organisation, and that meant Fenians and other advanced nationalists. The demand was simple: peasant proprietorship.

Parnell therefore found himself at the head of an organisation whose essential demand was revolutionary. In the summer of 1879, he already had good contacts with Fenians on both sides of the Atlantic and had their confidence. In 1879, a deal was agreed between the Supreme Council of the IRB – the Irish Republican Brotherhood, the formal name for the Fenians – and Parnell's supporters in the Home Rule Party. This was the so-called New Departure.

The New Departure meant the organisational and financial support of Fenianism for parliamentary action in return for the prosecution of new policies. First, there was to be a totally independent Irish party at Westminster without ties to any national British party and dedicated to Irish self-govern-

Land Legislation, 1870–1903

1870	Made customary tenant right enforceable at law and provided compensation for disturbance.
1881	Concession of the 'Three Fs': right of free sale; judicial power to fix rents; conversion of ordinary tenancies to fixed tenancies.
1885	Allowed land commission to lend to tenants to purchase holdings from landlords.
1903	Wyndham's Act. Provided for long-term low-interest government loans to buy out landlords' interests. This crucial piece of legislation effectively ended the land question and created the typical 20th-century pattern of independent family farms.

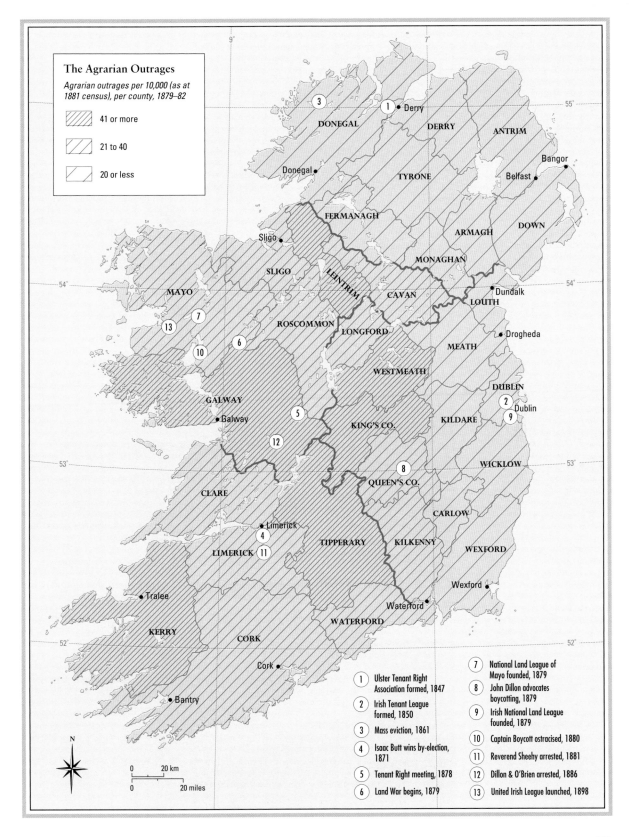

The Agrarian Outrages

Agrarian outrages per 10,000 (as at 1881 census), per county, 1879–82

41 or more

21 to 40

20 or less

DONEGAL

DERRY

• Derry

ANTRIM

Bangor •

TYRONE

Belfast •

Donegal •

FERMANAGH

ARMAGH

DOWN

Sligo •

SLIGO

LEITRIM

MONAGHAN

CAVAN

Dundalk •

LOUTH

MAYO

ROSCOMMON

LONGFORD

Drogheda •

MEATH

WESTMEATH

DUBLIN

GALWAY

• Galway

KING'S CO.

KILDARE

Dublin •

WICKLOW

CLARE

QUEEN'S CO.

CARLOW

• Limerick

LIMERICK

TIPPERARY

KILKENNY

WEXFORD

Tralee •

Wexford •

KERRY

CORK

WATERFORD

Waterford •

Cork •

Bantry •

1. Ulster Tenant Right Association formed, 1847
2. Irish Tenant League formed, 1850
3. Mass eviction, 1861
4. Isaac Butt wins by-election, 1871
5. Tenant Right meeting, 1878
6. Land War begins, 1879
7. National Land League of Mayo founded, 1879
8. John Dillon advocates boycotting, 1879
9. Irish National Land League founded, 1879
10. Captain Boycott ostracised, 1880
11. Reverend Sheehy arrested, 1881
12. Dillon & O'Brien arrested, 1886
13. United Irish League launched, 1898

N

0   20 km

0   20 miles

Avondale House, County Wicklow, the home of Charles Stewart Parnell.

ment. Butt's federal idea was to be scrapped. Second, the land agitation was to be brought to parliament in the form of a demand for legislation to create a peasant proprietorship.

By the autumn of 1880, the land war was in full swing. Across the country – except, significantly, in most of Ulster – agrarian protesters who previously had merely sought rent abatements in view of the recession were now demanding the abolition of the entire landlord system. Evictions were resisted by violence; where they occurred, revenge was taken on landlords either by attacks on themselves or their livestock; murders, burnings and boycotting increased.

The land war escalated into a wholesale attack on the landlords not just for what they were but for what they represented: the British connection. They were portrayed as a British garrison holding Ireland for the crown against the will of the people. The stakes were raised to the point where the social authority of the ascendancy was fatally wounded. The absolute communal solidarity of the tenants, under the leadership of the Land League, was now the key agent of social control. To take up a farm from which another had been evicted was to guarantee being boycotted (the word originated in the land war: the eponym was Capt Charles Boycott, a land agent in Co. Mayo). Land League courts effectively supplanted crown courts in many parts of rural Ireland.

Gladstone returned to power in 1880 and embarked on twin policy of coercion and conciliation. The use of special police powers to curb the excesses of the Land League was combined with a substantial concession to them. Gladstone's second Land Act – that of 1881 – conceded the 'Three Fs': the right of free sale by an outgoing tenant; fixity of tenure to replace ordinary tenancies; and a fixed rent to be determined by land courts. Parnell at first opposed the act on the grounds that it was not radical enough. The government lodged him in Kilmainham prison in Dublin whereupon rural crime escalated out of control. He was released as part of the 'Kilmainham Treaty', whereby he undertook to accept the act – with some cosmetic improvements – in return for using his influence to quell the agitation. The Kilmainham Treaty was an acknowledgement by the government that Parnell was, in the famous phrase, the uncrowned king of Ireland.

Even the hideous Phoenix Park murders of May 1882, less than a month after the Kilmainham Treaty, did not shake the new Gladstone-Parnell alliance. A group called the Invincibles – Fenian ultras – set upon Lord Frederick Cavendish, the new chief secretary of Ireland, and Thomas Burke, the undersecretary, as they were walking in the Phoenix Park in Dublin. Using surgical knives, they killed them both. Public opinion on both sides of the water was horrified. Parnell, fearing that his whole strategy was compromised, offered his resignation to Gladstone (not to his own party). Gladstone declined it.

The government outlawed the Land League, but the movement was already split between those who were happy with the new act and the radicals. Besides, Parnell was quite happy to see the end of the League, for in his eyes it had served its purpose. He himself, as might be expected of a landlord, was not an agrarian radical. He had ridden the tiger to a position of influence such as no one had had in Ireland since O'Connell. Its work was done and he was happy to dispense with it.

Besides, the Irish-American Fenian ultras spent much of the 1880s involved in a sporadic campaign of dynamite bombing in England. A 'skirmishing fund' was established to finance this activity, which in concept and method anticipated the IRA campaigns of a century later. The Tower of London, underground stations, Scotland Yard and even the chamber of the House of Commons itself were all targeted before the campaign was suppressed by the police in 1887. Among the many Fenians sentenced for their parts in this campaign was Thomas J. Clarke, destined to be the first signatory of the proclamation of the republic in 1916. The dynamite campaign was yet another reason for Parnell to distance himself from Fenian extremists while keeping mainstream Fenians safely on board the party ship.

He turned to the cause that really held his interest: home rule.

In October 1882, the organisation that succeeded the Land League was formed. Called the National League, it was firmly under Parnell's control; its purpose was to harness the mass support that had secured the 1881 Land Act for home rule and to act a constituency organisation for the Nationalist party, as we may now begin to call the home rule MPs.

The National League controlled the constituencies and the candidates chosen. Each candidate had to pledge to support and vote with the Nationalist party at Westminster, failing which he undertook to resign. Everything was centralised. Local particularism – never very subterranean in Ireland – was suppressed. At the apex of the entire structure was Parnell, the Chief. This structure was borrowed from Irish-American municipal politics, where ruthless discipline had delivered big-city administrations into Irish hands. The American Fenians who had insisted on an independent, pledge-bound party at Westminster as one of the terms of the New Departure knew what they were at. Tammany Hall came to the banks of the Thames.

The other key factor in the rise of the Nationalist party was its alliance with the Catholic church. This is one of those phenomena that seem perfectly natural in hindsight, but which were much more problematic in practice. First of all, Parnell was a Protestant. Second, he had close associations – to put it no stronger – with the Fenians, whom the church abominated as a revolutionary secret society after the French fashion. Third, he had exploited and profited from the Land League agitation, of which the church was deeply suspicious because of its subversion of the civic order.

On the other hand, it was clear that the Nationalists were an overwhelmingly Catholic party. Even in Butt's day a significant number of them had been loud champions of Catholic causes, most crucially that of denominational education. It was also clear that the National League was vastly more disciplined than the Land League had been. Dr Thomas Croke, the nationalist archbishop of Cashel, was an early supporter of Parnell. Others followed. The crucial alliance was forged in 1884, when the hierarchy agreed to throw the moral and organisational weight of the church behind the party; in return the party undertook to promote Catholic educational concerns in parliament.

Denominational education was a central concern of the church throughout the nineteenth century. The bishops founded a Catholic University in Dublin in 1854, with no less a person than Cardinal Newman as its first rector. It was the forerunner of UCD, now the country's biggest university. The hierarchy was determined to resist state interference in Catholic education at every level. The agreement between Parnell and the bishops meant that the party would act as a parliamentary watchdog in this matter.

The education question had acquired a greater importance since the Intermediate Education (Ireland) Act of 1878, which formalised the expansion of secondary education in the country. The system was centralised; state examinations were held; the state, through a newly established Education Board, assumed primary responsibility for financing the system. The emphasis was on a humanities-based academic curriculum. From the 1880s on this growing secondary system provided a ready supply of clerks, junior civil servants and – in the case of an elite minority – university undergraduates. In short, it laid the basis for the expansion of the Irish Catholic middle class. Like all open educational systems it generated a quiet revolution of rising expectations, the full effects of which would not be felt until 1916–22. Technical or vocational education – directed at working-class pupils, was less developed and followed only as a kind of afterthought at the turn of the century.

The general election of 1885 was the first to be fought under a greatly widened franchise introduced by act of parliament the previous year. In effect, the Representation of the People Act extended the vote to all male heads of households (except for a few statistically insignificant exceptions). Further legislation abolished most of the traditional borough constituencies – notoriously prone to corruption – and introduced a uniform constituency system. Ireland now had an electoral roll that was transformed at a stroke, rising from 226,000 to 738,000 persons. Unsurprisingly, the beneficiaries of this meritocratic extension of the vote were the populist parties on both the nationalist and unionist sides.

When the election results were declared, the Nationalists had won 86 seats and found themselves holding the balance of power in the House of Commons. After a brief tactical flirtation with the Conservatives, Parnell renewed the Liberal alliance. It was a telling moment. Parnell had always insisted on the absolute independence of the party. Now political realities were dictating otherwise. Henceforth, it was to be the Liberals or nothing. The price he extracted was the introduction of the first Irish Home Bill by Gladstone in 1886. It split the Liberal party and was defeated. The Liberals fell from power, not to return – except for a brief interlude in the early 1890s – for twenty years.

From the perspective of 1886, however, that was part of an unseen and unknown future. To contemporaries, Parnell has staged a stunning coup. A bill to create an Irish parliament to deal with domestic affairs had been sponsored on the floor of the House of Commons by the prime minister. Its defeat was less significant than the fact that it had happened at all. What had been unthinkable ten years earlier was now a central fact of political life. Like all great politicians, Parnell made the weather. The Irish Question was on the British agenda. It would remain there in one form or another until the 'solution' of 1920–22. Its aftershocks are there to the present day.

Of the 86 seats secured by the Nationalists in the 1885 election, 17 were in Ulster. This represented a simple majority of the province's 33 seats. The other 16 were all Conservatives. Ulster Liberalism was destroyed at the polls. Tenants on either side of the sectarian divide who had previously voted Liberal now chose the Conservatives (if Protestant) to defend the union or Nationalist (if Catholic) to subvert it. Politics in the province took on the reductive form it has had ever since: for or against the union.

Combined with Gladstone's conversion to home rule, this was the moment of truth for Ulster Protestants. They mobilised a pan-Protestant movement in defence of the union. They feared that what they regarded as the backward, agricultural, Catholic south would overwhelm the progressive, industrial, Protestant north. Confessional and material self-interest dovetailed neatly.

Ulster Conservatives now moved closer to the Orange Order, with its tradition of cross-class popular mobilisation. Borrowing freely from nationalist techniques, they organised a series of mass meetings across the province culminating in a mass rally in the Ulster Hall in Belfast on 22 February 1886. The principal speaker was Lord Randolph Churchill, the dazzlingly unstable younger son of the Duke of Marlborough and father of Winston. Churchill's formula, 'Ulster will fight, and Ulster will be right' became a rallying cry for Ulster Protestants.

The defeat of the Home Rule Bill two months later seemed like a deliverance. The return of the Conservatives under Lord Salisbury removed the immediate danger but the crisis had changed the political landscape in Ulster forever.

The tensions surrounding the home rule crisis tripped off the worst sectarian rioting that Belfast had yet seen. From June to September, the riots went on sporadically leaving an official death count of 31, although unofficial estimates suggested nearer 50. Belfast was, more than ever before, a city divided absolutely along sectarian lines. In this, it reflected the wider Ulster reality which was

Castle Street, Belfast

determined by the delicate confessional demography of the province.

The franchise extension that proved so important in the elections of 1885 was in many ways just the reflection of a developing public opinion, a widening of the public sphere. The transport revolution effected by the ever-expanding railway system had united different parts of the island in a manner previously unthinkable. It also provided the distribution system for national newspapers, which acquired a growing importance. The two most venerable Irish papers, the *Belfast Newsletter* and the *Freeman's Journal*, dating from 1737 and 1763 respectively, could now expand beyond their traditional readership base in Belfast and Dublin. The *Freeman*, in particular, became the most important voice of nationalist Ireland, so much so that during the Parnell split of 1890–91 both sides tried hard to seize control of it. A national newspaper furnished its community with a common agenda, a common rhetoric and grammar, a common pulpit for the dissemination of political and social views. It was a force for national integration as distinct from local particularism. As such, the expansion of the national press in the second half of the nineteenth century was a key development.

It reflected the growing literacy rate in Ireland. The 1841 census estimated that fewer than half of those aged five or more could read. By the census of 1911, the figure had risen to 88 per cent. The wholesale destruction of the poorest classes in the Famine, whether through death or emigration, together with the steady expansion of the education system, had accounted for this impressive increase. The newspapers therefore had a viable customer base as well as an efficient distribution system. *The Irish Times* was founded in 1859, mainly as the voice of southern unionism. From 1905 on the *Freeman* was increasingly challenged by the new *Irish Independent*, destined to become the leading organ of lower middle-class nationalism in the twentieth century. *The Cork Examiner* dated from 1841: technically it was classed as a national newspaper, although it was never strong outside its regional base in Munster.

The development of a national press was paralleled by the equally impressive and important growth of local newspapers, most of them unapologetically partisan in their politics. *The Munster Express*, published in Waterford, dates from 1859. The first edition of the *Leinster Leader* announced itself in 1881 as the voice of the nationalist community in Co. Kildare. *The Limerick Leader* (1889) declared itself to be 'a faithful organ of the National Party'. In all, it was estimated that the number of provincial papers increased from 68 in 1850 to more than 120 by the 1880s. The number of overtly nationalist newspapers published outside Dublin grew from zero in 1861 to 34 in 1891. Newspaper proprietors and editors were important and influential figures within the overall nationalist movement.

As with nationalism, so with unionism. *The Belfast Telegraph* dates from 1870. Two of the most important local Ulster papers that championed the unionist cause date from the 1820s, the *Impartial Reporter* (surely one of the least apposite titles in the history of journalism) in the marchland of Co. Fermanagh and the *Londonderry Sentinel*. These early foundation dates reflect the high literacy rates of Ulster Protestants (especially Presbyterians) as well as anxiety at the growth of O'Connellism. Their effect among unionists was similar to that of their nationalist equivalents: they provided a forum for news and debate, and therefore furnished the means to create an integrated political community.

To Parnell and the Nationalists, the defeat of the Home Rule Bill seemed just a temporary setback. The immense prestige of Gladstone lay behind the

The O'Connell Century Celebrations, 1875 painted by Charles Russell.

cause; Parnell's reputation had never stood higher; it seemed only a matter of time before the natural pendulum of British politics would restore the Liberals to power and home rule to the political agenda.

In 1889 *The Times* falsely accused Parnell of conspiring with the Invincibles in the Phoenix Park Murders of 1882 and of approving the deaths of Cavendish and Burke. The whole thing was based on the forgeries of one Richard Pigott. A commission of inquiry exposed the fraud, leaving Parnell's public position stronger than ever. On his return to the Commons, he got a standing ovation from all sides. He was just 43 years of age, at the height of his powers, adored in nationalist Ireland, respected at Westminster, the undisputed leader of a nation-in-waiting. It was this that made his fall so shocking.

For many years, Parnell had lived with Katharine O'Shea, the estranged wife of Capt William O'Shea MP. O'Shea had squandered an inheritance and proved an incompetent businessman before entering politics in 1880. He lost his seat in 1885. He knew of the affair between Parnell and his wife and tolerated it. He could not afford to sue for divorce, since he was dependent for financial support on an elderly aunt of Katherine's who would have been scandalised by such a course. She eventually died, at which point Willie O'Shea's inhibitions deserted him. He sued for divorce, citing his wife's adultery and naming Parnell as co-respondent.

Amazingly, nationalist solidarity held. The Catholic bishops clearly disapproved of the behaviour of the Protestant adulterer but stayed their hand. The parliamentary party prepared to re-elect Parnell as leader. It was at this point that elements in the Liberal party withdrew their support for Parnell. The nonconformist conscience was being exercised.

There was a strong element of Christian moral earnestness in some Liberals' support for home rule: Gladstone himself was animated by it. Now these Liberals were telling Gladstone that Parnell's continued leadership of the Nationalist party would subvert the Liberal alliance. He was in their eyes a morally unfit person. Gladstone was now faced with either sacrificing Parnell or losing the leadership of Liberalism. He presented the Nationalists with a hideous dilemma. They could have Parnell or the Liberal alliance but not both.

The party split on 15 December 1890. The majority chose the Liberals. Parnell attempted to reconstruct his political fortunes in a series of three bitterly fought by-election campaigns in Ireland over the following year, all of which he lost. The church, determined not to be out moralised by a crowd of English Protestants, turned against him. The Split was a savage business, with passions inflamed beyond reason on both sides. It darkened Irish nationalist life for a generation.

Parnell's frenzied by-election campaigns killed him. Never robust, he was

drenched to the skin while addressing a meeting in Creggs, Co. Roscommon and caught a chill which developed into pneumonia. He dragged himself back to Brighton, where he lived with Katharine, and died there on 6 October 1891. His remains were returned to Dublin where his funeral attracted over 100,000 mourners. He is buried in the most impressive grave in Ireland, in Glasnevin cemetery under a single boulder of Wicklow granite bearing the simple legend PARNELL.

Parnell's grave, Glasnevin Cemetery.

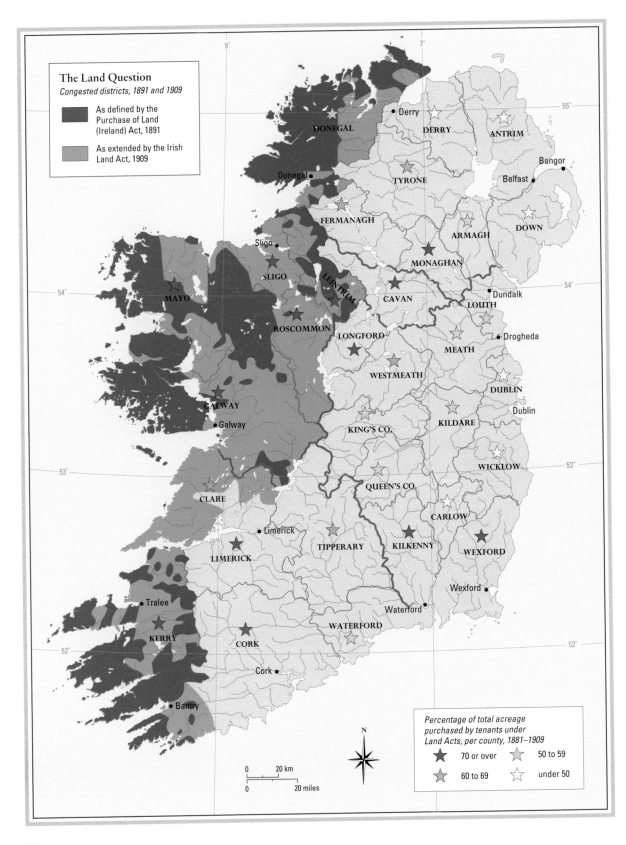

The Land Question
Congested districts, 1891 and 1909

As defined by the Purchase of Land (Ireland) Act, 1891

As extended by the Irish Land Act, 1909

Percentage of total acreage purchased by tenants under Land Acts, per county, 1881–1909

70 or over
60 to 69
50 to 59
under 50

CHAPTER 8

LONG GESTATION
The Cultural Revival 1891–1912

Parnell was dead. The party was split between the anti-Parnellite majority and the Parnellite minority. The 1890s was a wretched decade for Irish nationalist politics. The Nationalists eventually reunited in 1900 under the leadership of John Redmond, who had headed the Parnellite faction. The assumption of the leadership by someone from the smaller group was a conscious attempt to bind up wounds. But while the party gradually recovered its sense of purpose, it never regained the iron unity and discipline of Parnell's day.

In the meantime, the Conservative governments of Lord Salisbury resumed their policy of 'killing home rule with kindness'. This meant social and economic reforms and initiatives designed to prove that good government was better than self-government. The policy had first been articulated under an earlier Tory government in the late 1880s and early 1890s. The then chief secretary, Arthur Balfour, had established the Congested Districts Board in 1891 to assist in development schemes for the poorer parts of the country – mainly along the Atlantic seaboard. The initiatives included infrastructural developments: many of the country's quaint narrow-gauge railways were financed by the board. Harbours were constructed. Cottage crafts and education in modern agricultural methods were encouraged.

Land War poster.

The Local Government Act of 1898 modernised an antique system, sweeping away grand juries and poor law boards and establishing democratically elected county councils and urban councils. This had the important effect of making numbers count at local level, replacing unionists with nationalists in most cases. Many stalwarts of the Irish revolution first cut their political teeth in these local assemblies.

The most momentous piece of legislation came in 1903, when the chief secretary, George Wyndham, introduced the Land Act that has ever since borne his name. The Conservatives had long been of the view that a move to tenant purchase was the solution to the land question, which had flared up intermittently ever since the suppression of the Land League.

119

The 1903 Act provided government funds to buy out the Irish landlords and transfer the land to the former tenants who now became independent proprietors. Thus the independent family farm came to pass. The act resulted from a conference at which all interests had been represented, so it was a consensual piece of legislation. This was a remarkable achievement, considering the mayhem in the countryside a mere twenty years earlier. The purchasers were given long-term loans by the government. The repayments, over thirty-five years, generally annualised at a lower figure than the old rents. From the landlords' point of view, payments were in cash rather than bonds and the government offered a 12 per cent premium for estates that were sold in their entirety.

No piece of legislation in any parliament has had such a transforming effect on the country. It was the moment of triumph for the former tenants, who were now established not just as proprietors but soon would be the most significant social group in the country. Now they were an interest, no longer a cause: one of the ironies of their triumph is that the Nationalist party no longer had its core issue to rally and unite it. The land question was effectively settled.

Anti-Rent meeting in Limerick.

Although few realised it at the time, the Fenian moment was at hand. The paralysis of parliamentary nationalism offered an opening to a group that had been overshadowed by Parnell for a decade. The Fenians had represented a kind of internal opposition within the larger nationalist tent. They were a radical ginger group. As a movement with particularly strong transatlantic connections, they had access to money and expertise. Their membership was drawn disproportionately from lower middle-class town dwellers of the south and east, so that they were an identifiable social sub-group in a nationalist movement that was still overwhelmingly rural and whose great populist integrating cause was land reform. Indeed, the Fenians were chary of the whole land agitation, partly because they were townies and partly because many of them were themselves property owners in a small way and sensitive to the rights of property. Ideologically, they distrusted the land agitation as a distraction from what they regarded as the only clear goal appropriate to nationalist ambition: separation from Britain.

None the less, they had survived the fiasco of 1867 and still had enough vigour to mount the London dynamite campaign of the 1880s. Despite their doubts about the Land League, they had played an important role in its success: as we saw, American Fenians were crucial in securing the New Departure of 1879 that effectively set the Land League in motion. Fenianism was as much a mood, a temperamental disposition, as anything else. Its adherents were usually better educated than the general run of the population. Many possessed tough, assertive personalities. They had good organisational skills and were to be found at the radical cutting edge of most nationalist movements. They insinuated themselves into Parnell's movement – although Parnell had the measure of them after 1882 – and were prominent in agitations such as the Plan of Campaign, an attempt in the late 1880s to revive the agrarian radicalism of the earlier years of the decade. Police reports identified them as shopkeepers and publicans, commercial travellers, auctioneers, journalists and such like. In short, they were men of modest substance and some education. They had ambitions. They had ideas. They dreamed dreams. They were an ideal revolutionary class. And from the 1890s on, they are everywhere.

Every significant cultural and social movement in nationalist Ireland after the fall of Parnell had its Fenian presence. Indeed, as we see below, the Gaelic Athletic Association was almost an exclusively Fenian enterprise. The great irony was that the activity which the Fenians despised and at which they appeared to be no use – politics – was eventually where they were to have their greatest triumph. But all that lay in the future. In the meantime, there was organic work to be done and myths to be made.

In 1893, the Gaelic League was formed. The founder was Eoin Mac Néill, an historian of early and medieval Ireland. The first president was Douglas Hyde, the son of a Church of Ireland rector from Co. Roscommon. A scholar and linguist, he had delivered a lecture in 1892 under the title 'The Necessity for De-anglicising the Irish People', in which he called for an arrest in the decline of the Irish language and deplored the advance of what he regarded as a vulgar, English commercial culture.

Early premises of Conradh na Gaeilge (the Gaelic League) in Sackville Street, around the turn of the century.

The new organisation established itself quickly. It had as its aim the revival of Irish as the common vernacular. It conducted language classes. It published stories, plays and a newspaper, *An Claidheamh Soluis* (The Sword of Light). It opposed a campaign led by Mahaffy, the Provost of Trinity College Dublin, to have the language removed from the Intermediate school syllabus. It established language teacher training colleges. By 1908, there 600 branches of the League around the country.

An Claideam Soluir

[AN CLAIDHEAMH SOLUIS.]
„ᵅᵹᵘᵣ Fáinne an Laᵹ. „

[REGISTERED AS A NEWSPAPER.]

Leabar V. Uimir 14.
Vol. V.   No. 14.

baile ára cliat, meiteam 13, 1903.
DUBLIN, JUNE 13, 1903.

pinginn.
One Penny.

Cúrraí an t-Saoᵹail

Sᵹéala ó na Cúiᵹ Cúiᵹi.

IAR-Çonnaċta.

Saor-Ceappaireaċt Gaeveaᵹaċ.

— Feir loċ ᵹarmain. —

Droiċeav Cromil.

"I SY, old dame, can you tell me where Cromwell's Bridge is?"

"Cromil's Bridge, is it? I can that thin. Go down into the lowest depths o' the blackest pits o' Hell—there you'll find Cromil an' his bridges too."

Sruaᵹáċ an tobair.

bille na talman.

The Gaelic League successfully revived the Young Irelanders' idea that cultural and linguistic autonomy was a good thing, and was part of a greater national revival. Hyde naively thought that the language was a non-political issue on which people of all religious and social backgrounds could meet without rancour. The League was indeed non-political for the first twenty-two years of its life. But its implied purpose was clear: the re-Gaelicisation of Ireland. In some ways, it was a very Victorian phenomenon, appealing to the same kind of medieval nostalgia that animated the pre-Raphaelites and the arts and crafts movement in England.

By injecting a strong cultural element into the national mix, the Gaelic League was part of a larger movement that developed from the 1890s onwards. What is commonly called the Irish Literary Revival was the work of a remarkable generation of writers and intellectuals. It is often represented as a reaction to the sordid politics of the Parnell split and a search for a more honourable and positive means of expressing national sentiment. Certainly, W. B. Yeats thought so. Many years later, when making his acceptance speech in Stockholm upon winning the Nobel Prize for Literature he declared unambiguously:

'The modern literature of Ireland, and indeed all that stir of thought which prepared for the Anglo-Irish war, began when Parnell fell from power in 1891. A disillusioned and embittered Ireland turned away from parliamentary politics; an event was conceived and the race began, as I think, to be troubled by that event's long gestation.'

The literary revival – indeed the whole cultural revival of which it was the most distinguished part – drew inspiration from the Young Ireland poets associated with *The Nation* as well as from the work of antiquarians and Celtic scholars in Ireland and on the continent. Like all such movements, it required a central figure. It found it in Yeats.

Yeats was not simply a poet of genius but also a very considerable man of action. He had started publishing in the late 1880s and continued in the following decade. His influential Celtic Twilight collection appeared in 1893 and gave the entire movement a name that stuck. Yeats was fascinated by mysticism and eastern religion and managed to translate both to a Celtic locale. He shared this enthusiasm with many leading figures in the movement, most notably the remarkable George Russell (AE), and in temper the literary movement was hostile to mere rational modernity.

It was also, to a remarkable degree for a movement of its kind, Protestant. Yeats, Russell and Lady Gregory, the patron and eminence grise of the movement, were all Protestants. So were Synge and O'Casey, its two great dramatists, and many of its minor figures. It has been speculated that they represented an enlightened Protestant vanguard, aware that the game was up for the old

Opposite: The front page of an early edition of An Claidheamh Soluis, *the newspaper of the Gaelic League.*

order with the disestablishment of the Church of Ireland and the end of the estate system, and anxious to find a role and make a stamp on the new Ireland.

The Gaelic League and the literary revival overlapped in places and shared a common sensibility. Both were anti-utilitarian and romantic. This brought both movements, but especially the literary revival, onto a collision course with the very utilitarian Catholic middle class. This group was the backbone of actual, living nationalist society. It had little interest in mystic speculation, although its national pride was flattered by the dramatic representation of Irish heroic myths. Yeats's play, *Cathleen Ni Houlihan*, first given in Dublin in 1902, was a thinly disguised call to arms against England and famously gave the poet qualms of conscience in later years.

Yeats was many things, including a Fenian sympathiser (perhaps even an actual Fenian for a while) but was consistent in his distaste for the middle class. His thoroughly reactionary dream of a union of aristocrats and peasants against the philistine bourgeoisie left no place for the very people who were inheriting the new nationalist world that was forming all about him. The farmers, shopkeepers, clerks and others of this sort who had been the backbone of Parnell's party had other voices to articulate their concerns and prejudices: voices like those of the brilliantly waspish lawyer and parliamentarian Tim Healy – the most eloquently vituperative of the anti-Parnellites – and D.P. Moran, a journalist with a supreme talent for abuse. His journal, *The Leader*, founded in 1900, was a scabrously entertaining cocktail of lower-middle class nationalist prejudice against Protestants, intellectuals, the English, the rich, nationalists like Arthur Griffith of whom Moran did not approve, and anything and anyone that caught the editor's ire. Moran was a bottomless pit of acid.

Yeats's world and Moran's collided in 1907 when Synge's *Playboy of the Western World* opened at the Abbey. Yeats and Lady Gregory had founded the theatre three years earlier: it was one of the monumental achievements of the revival. Patriotic plays were one thing. The gritty realism of Synge was another. The *Playboy* is set in Co. Mayo and the peasant cast is presented, in part at least, as ignorant, credulous and superstitious. This was deeply offensive to a nationalist audience, which saw only stage-Irish caricature. They also shared the prissy puritanism of the age, so that when a reference was made to a 'shift' – a lady's undergarment or slip – it was the trigger for an already shocked and tense audience to riot.

The Playboy riot was not simply a contest between art and philistinism, although this was naturally the myth that Yeats made of it. It was a collision of different mental worlds. Ironically, both were attempting a definition of Irishness and its place in the world that was transforming. For the utilitarian middle class, virtue meant material progress, piety, respectability and move-

Aerial view of the Aran Islands.

ment towards home rule. Indeed, if you subtract the political element, the nationalist middle class had aspirations very similar to their counterparts in the rest of the United Kingdom. After the trauma of the Famine, less than a life-time before, the advance in material fortunes was a source of pride. Synge's peasants seemed like some sort of pre-Famine horror, drawn by a condescending Protestant in a theatre run by the widow of Sir William Gregory – he of the Famine quarter-acre clause.

For Yeats and Synge, the autonomy of great art and its fidelity to reality was the supreme virtue. Part of the problem for the audience was precisely that Synge was not drawing stage-Irish characters: they were all too real. Synge had spent many nights in western cottages, listening and noting the vocabulary, syntax and cadences of western peasants. It was his fidelity in reproducing their speech – these people who were now a social embarrassment to the new bourgeoisie – that was troubling. Set in the context of a powerful psychological drama, a truly stirring work of art, the tension proved too great.

That tension was caused by a gap between politics and culture in national-

Hurling, the quintessential Irish Sport. Munster Senior Hurling Championship, semi-final 28 May 2006.

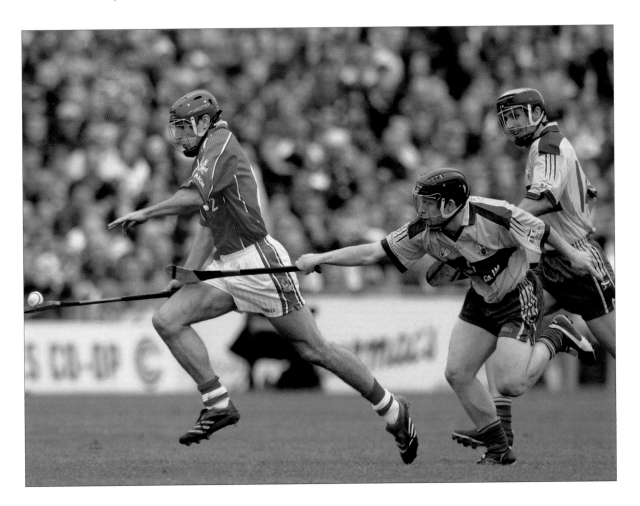

ist Ireland that nothing could bridge in the early twentieth century. Nationalist politics had focused on the material, most obviously on the land question. Its organisational methods were borrowed from Tammany Hall and were not for the squeamish. It was hand in glove with the Catholic clergy. It was careful and calculating. The cultural revival occurred after O'Connell and Parnell had set the material template for nationalism. It now attempted to overlay a cultural template and to furnish nationalism with myths and symbols. In this, it had considerable success but its sensibility was always at an oblique angle to the utilitarianism of the political and social mainstream. Unlike many other European nationalisms, where the culture came first and the politics second, in Ireland it was the other way round. In the end, as Yeats would discover, the politics would crush the culture, demanding of it a role subservient to the wishes and prejudices of the new dominant class. Nationalism cannibalised the cultural revival for those titbits it could digest. It rejected the rest.

If the Gaelic League attempted to stay non-political, the other key cultural organisation of the period from the Parnell split to the Easter Rising had no such inhibitions. On the contrary, the Gaelic Athletic Association was a Fenian vehicle from the start. It has also been the most successful popular association in modern Irish history.

It was founded in Thurles, Co. Tipperary in 1884. Its purpose was to preserve and promote the ancient game of hurling. In addition, it developed a code of football which went on to become the most popular spectator sport in twentieth-century Ireland. For the Fenians, it offered a perfect recruiting vehicle and its politics reflected Fenian radicalism right from the beginning. It was aggressively Parnellite at the time of the split and thereafter was to be found on the left of the nationalist movement on every occasion. It was republican in politics; hugely supportive of the Irish language and of Gaelic culture in general; tacitly Catholic, although not clerical, in its assumptions; and ferociously opposed to the symbols of British rule, not least the police. It imposed a ban on its members playing 'foreign games' – defined as soccer, rugby, hockey and cricket – which lasted until 1971.

In part, it was a reaction against the exclusiveness of other sports. Rugby was focused on elite private schools; cricket had a long association with both army and ascendancy; athletics was administered by a Trinity College elite which discouraged, to put it no more strongly, the participation of the wrong sort of chaps. The GAA was perfect for the people whose faces did not fit. To be fair, this point can easily be exaggerated: there is much local evidence from the late 1880s, when things were still fluid, that GAA clubs were founded by athletes who cheerfully played cricket and association football (soccer). The exclusiveness was not all one way: the ban on foreign games was also a form of exclusion, a kind of recreational tariff wall willed by the Fenian element in the GAA for political-cultural reasons.

At any rate, the GAA became the great popular mobilising force in Irish recreational life. And it did so in a context that applauded exclusion, that insisted on the separateness of Gaelic games and the social life that revolved around them. Matches were played on Sundays, the only free day in the working week, which guaranteed that sabbatarian Protestants were unlikely to participate. The GAA soon spread to every Catholic parish in the country, with a local club often named for a saint or a patriot: thus Naomh (Saint) this-or-that, plus various Emmets, Tones, Sarsfields and so on. There were few named for O'Connell, whose aversion to violence made him persona non grata in Fenian eyes. This was ironic, given that its organisational structure so clearly mirrored O'Connell's own.

The GAA, the most Fenian and anglophobe of all nationalist organisations, was also a very modern phenomenon. The codification of sports – a mid-Victorian phenomenon – meant the establishment of uniform rules for a game

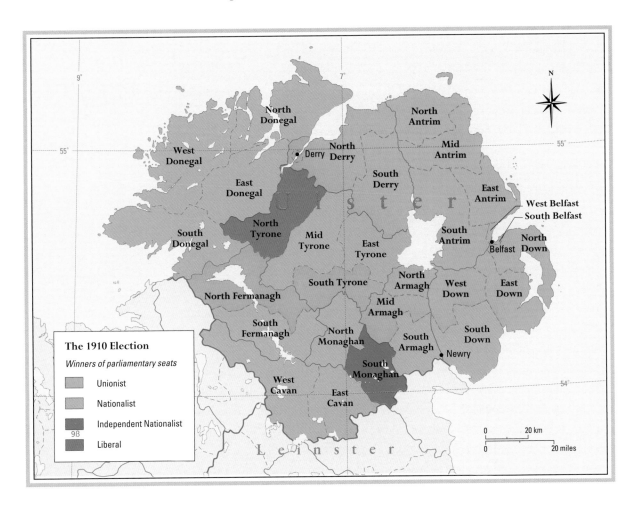

The 1910 Election

Winners of parliamentary seats

Unionist

Nationalist

Independent Nationalist

Liberal

from a multitude of regional variants. Their antecedents of soccer and rugby were local rough-and-tumbles with local rules. Cricket had a number of regional antecedents like stoolball (which could have as easily evolved into baseball as into cricket). Eventually, cricket was codified on the rules of the game as played in Kent, Surrey and Hampshire. The West Country and Yorkshire variations now had to accommodate themselves to the new national standard. In baseball, the New York game displaced rival versions such as town ball and the so-called Massachusetts game. All this was a product of the railway revolution, which made national championships possible for the first time, and therefore led to a requirement for a uniform set of rules.

The codification of hurling followed a similar path. The game had been particularly popular in three areas in pre-Famine times: in south Leinster and east Munster; on either side of the middle reaches of the Shannon, where east Galway looks across to south Offaly and north-west Tipperary; and in the Glens of Antrim. The Famine dealt what was nearly a death blow to the game in the first two areas: indeed, cricket waxed strong in these areas in the post-Famine years.

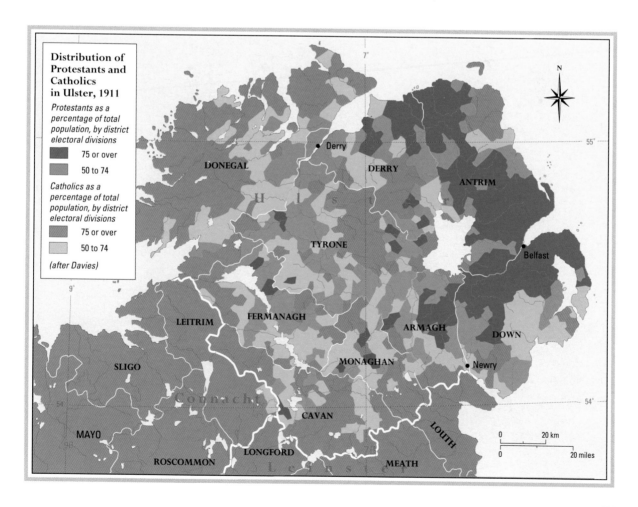

It was the need to revive hurling that inspired the founders of the association.

And revive it they did. But in codifying the game they faced a problem. The game played in the Glens of Antrim was significantly different to the southern game. Unsurprisingly, given the ancient association between Antrim and the west of Scotland (the Mull of Kintyre is plainly visible from the Antrim coast on a fine day), the game played there was closer to Scottish shinty. The two games, while clearly related, have very obvious differences.

Modern hurling was codified along the lines of the South Leinster game. Antrim had to adjust accordingly if it was to participate at national level. This interesting little exercise in internal imperialism was typical of how most sports were codified. The GAA may have been exclusive and different, but it obeyed the logic of all national sporting associations engaged in similar exercises.

The 1890s was the decade in which culture displaced politics in Ireland. The material conditions for the triumph of Irish nationalism had been progressively consolidated in the course of the nineteenth century. Now it was time to develop enabling tribal myths. It was in these years, from the fall of Parnell to

Early 1900s Orange Parade, Ulster.

the outbreak of the Great War, that so many forces coalesced to furnish the tribe with a flattering narrative. Wyndham's Land Act created an independent yeomanry. The GAA epitomised simple athleticism and courage, bringing to physical life the myth of rural virtue conjured up in *Knocknagow*, a sprawling sentimental novel from the pen of the Fenian Charles Kickham. The cultural revival proposed the rural poor of the western seaboard – especially the Irish-speaking remnant – as a vision of authenticity towards which the rest of the nation should aspire. For the first two-thirds of the twentieth century, the *beau ideal* of Irishness was the Irish-speaking western small holder: it was this vision of sober, Jeffersonian rectitude that Eamon de Valera famously celebrated in 1943 when he spoke of 'that Ireland which we dreamed of'.

It was, indeed, a dream but one possessed of great vitality and imaginative force. It was always in collision with material and instrumental reality, which gave it a certain kind of intellectual weightlessness, but myths can be as important as realities in the making of nations and states. Nowhere was the delusional aspect of the cultural revival more complete than in the matter of the Irish language, aspiration and sociology in violent collision as the vernacular numbers dropped in every generation. Yet the revival of Irish has been a central feature of Irish public policy throughout the twentieth century and into the twenty-first. It remains a compulsory school subject in the Republic and, despite occasional low-level grousing, still commands overwhelming sentimental affection. It is still thought of as 'our language' when plainly the quotidian evidence is that it is not.

If the material conditions for nationalism had been established, so had those for partition. The unforgiving sectarian geography of Ulster was made plain in the 1885 election – the first fought under a sufficiently wide franchise to be truly representative and democratic. It has been confirmed in every test of public opinion in Ulster for more than a century. The more strident and insistent has been the nationalist demand, the more unyielding and sullen has been the unionist resistance. Look at the map (p. 129) showing the distribution of Protestants and Catholics in Ulster in 1911: the point where Catholic numbers weaken and Protestants begin to appear in strength is roughly where the line of partition was drawn in 1920. And within what became Northern Ireland, there was already a clear east-west divide between the Protestant heartland in the east (only counties Derry, Antrim and Down had Protestant majorities) and the local Catholic majority west of the River Bann.

The Irish *fin de siècle* was therefore the time when the twin forces that would dominate the island in the coming century took definitive form: the full realisation of the nationalist self-image and the boundary of the unionist redoubt.

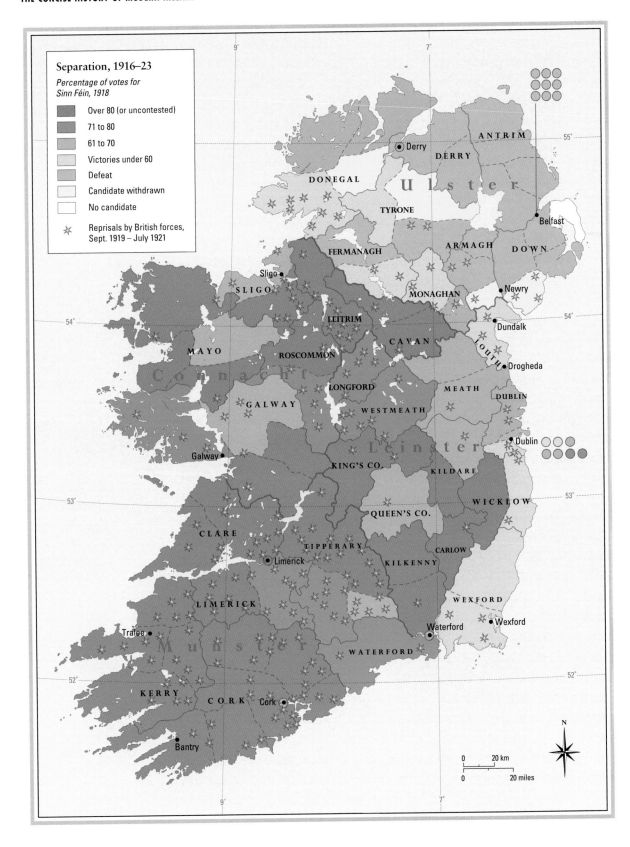

Separation, 1916–23

Percentage of votes for Sinn Féin, 1918

- Over 80 (or uncontested)
- 71 to 80
- 61 to 70
- Victories under 60
- Defeat
- Candidate withdrawn
- No candidate

✳ Reprisals by British forces, Sept. 1919 – July 1921

CHAPTER 9

THE IRISH REVOLUTION
Rebellion, Partition and Civil War
1912–23

The political flux following the Parnell split produced a situation in which radical and maverick groups flourished. The one that endured was Sinn Féin, founded in 1905. In Irish, Sinn Féin means 'ourselves', not 'ourselves alone' as it is sometimes mistranslated. The point is worth emphasising, because the mistranslation suggests a degree of separatist purity which the early Sinn Féin simply did not possess. Its emphasis was on economic and cultural self-reliance. Its leading figure, Arthur Griffith, was not himself a republican. He espoused a dual monarchy along the lines of the Austro-Hungarian settlement of 1867. It is not hard to see how an emphasis on national self-reliance was easily compatible with separatism and republicanism, but Sinn Féin prior to 1916 was by no means wedded to either doctrine. It was, however, close enough in sympathy to those who were to fool the British, who dubbed the 1916 rising the 'Sinn Féin rebellion'. As we shall see, Sinn Féin had nothing to do with 1916, but the name stuck none the less.

Arthur Griffith.

It is important not to exaggerate the importance of the early Sinn Féin. It was simply the most prominent of a number of radical nationalist groups, both in the political and cultural spheres. The later centrality of Sinn Féin should not blind us to its marginality in the first decade of the twentieth century. Especially after the return of the Liberals to power in Westminster in 1905, the Nationalist party's fortunes began to improve. There was, however, one key difference between Parnell's party and Redmond's. Parnell embraced the Fenians and contained them within the party structure. Redmond never had them securely on board. Until 1912 or so, this did not seem to matter. After 1916, it was fatal to Redmond's fortunes.

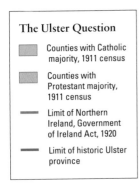

The Ulster Question

Counties with Catholic majority, 1911 census

Counties with Protestant majority, 1911 census

Limit of Northern Ireland, Government of Ireland Act, 1920

Limit of historic Ulster province

The 1910 election produced a hung parliament and, sure enough, the Liberal leader Asquith could only form a government with Redmond's support. Home rule was back on the agenda. In April 1912, the third Home Rule Bill was introduced in the House of Commons. After ferocious Conservative opposition, it was not carried until January 1913. Predictably, it was then defeated in the Lords. However, the Parliament Act of 1911 had removed the Lords' veto, replacing it with a delaying power of two years. This meant that home rule would become a reality in 1914. The 1912 bill was Redmond's apotheosis. Parnell's dream, it seemed, was about to come true. Except, of course, that it never did.

In March 1905, the Ulster Unionist Council was formed in Belfast. Northern unionists had been alarmed at the conciliatory manner of their southern counterparts during the negotiations that preceded the Land Act of 1903. The differences between southern and northern unionism were clear. In the south, the remnants of the old ascendancy were reduced in fortune, land and prestige. In the north, a self-confident commercial aristocracy had been created by the industrial revolution.

The formation of the UUC announced the end of intra-Protestant rivalry and the creation of a communal solidarity that reflected that on the nationalist, Catholic side. Given the fractious nature of Protestantism, with its emphasis on individual conscience and judgment, this was a more difficult task than it seemed. Indeed, the kind of organisational unity represented by the UUC was easiest to sustain in times of crisis. When the crisis passed or abated, the underlying tensions resurfaced.

The real crisis for Ulster unionism came with the introduction of the third Home Rule bill. With the power of the Lords now emasculated, it meant that victory in the Commons would be enough to force the measure through. The bill was anathema to all unionists.

The unionists had four advantages in their opposition to home rule: first, they were passionate about it and prepared to go to any extreme to win; second, they had a local majority in their Ulster heartland; third, they had the

John Redmond.

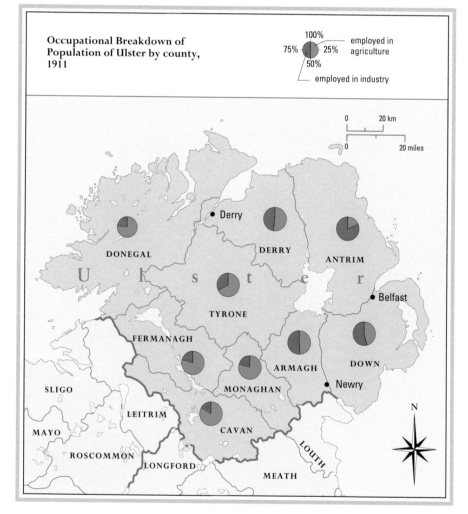

Occupational Breakdown of Population of Ulster by county, 1911

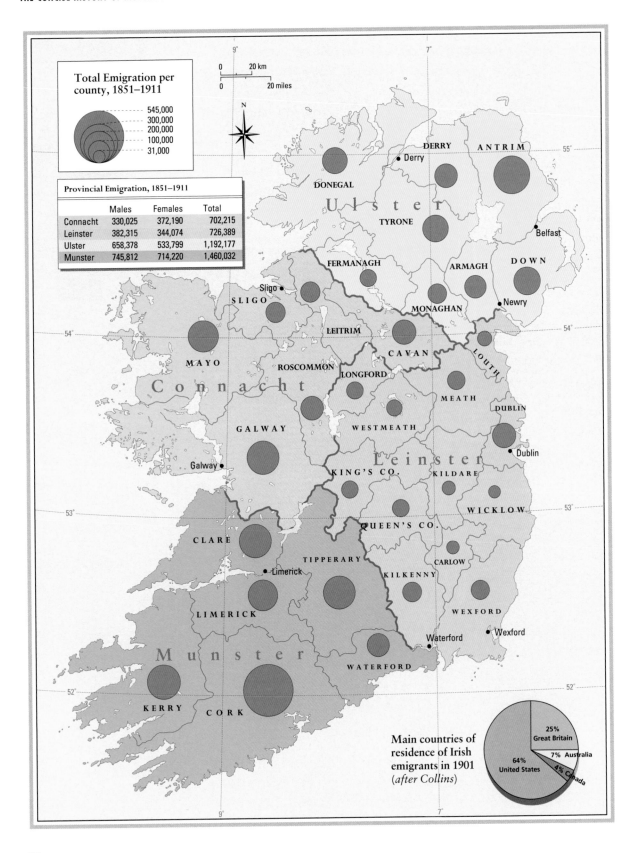

Total Emigration per county, 1851–1911

545,000
300,000
200,000
100,000
31,000

Provincial Emigration, 1851–1911			
	Males	Females	Total
Connacht	330,025	372,190	702,215
Leinster	382,315	344,074	726,389
Ulster	658,378	533,799	1,192,177
Munster	745,812	714,220	1,460,032

20 km

20 miles

N

Ulster

DERRY
• Derry

ANTRIM

DONEGAL

TYRONE

• Belfast

FERMANAGH

ARMAGH

DOWN

MONAGHAN

• Newry

Sligo •

SLIGO

LEITRIM

CAVAN

LOUTH

MAYO

ROSCOMMON

LONGFORD

MEATH

DUBLIN

Connacht

WESTMEATH

GALWAY

• Dublin

Leinster

Galway •

KING'S CO.

KILDARE

WICKLOW

CLARE

QUEEN'S CO.

TIPPERARY

CARLOW

• Limerick

KILKENNY

LIMERICK

WEXFORD

Munster

WATERFORD

• Wexford

Waterford •

KERRY

CORK

Main countries of residence of Irish emigrants in 1901 (*after Collins*)

25% Great Britain

7% Australia

64% United States

4% Canada

enthusiastic support of the Conservative party in Britain; finally, they had two leaders of real ability.

Edward Carson became leader of the UUC in 1910. Born in Dublin, he was a barrister in London, where his most celebrated performance had been in the destruction of Oscar Wilde at his trial in 1895. Carson was a commanding and rather mercurial figure, who brought immense prestige and good Conservative connections to the Ulster cause. In fact, the cause for him was that of Irish unionism *tout court*, although the focus was essentially on Ulster. He was in the O'Connell-Parnell mould of Irish leader, urging radicalism and mass mobilisation to squeeze concessions from London. For that, he needed a mass movement. James Craig, a hatchet-faced millionaire typical of the new money plutocracy, gave it to him.

A series of meetings and rallies and an effective publicity campaign ensured that public opinion in Protestant Ulster was thoroughly mobilised. The campaign culminated in Ulster Day, 28 September 1912, with the signing of Ulster's Solemn League and Covenant by almost a quarter of a million men. This document or pledge was a conscious echo of the Solemn League and Covenant of 1643, in which Scots Presbyterians and English parliamentarians had united against the government of King Charles I. The historical parallel of united opposition to overweening authority was irresistible. The whole exercise was a brilliant *coup de theatre*.

It became clear to the government that some concession would have to be made to Ulster opinion, as the popular campaign grew ever more shrill. But any concession to unionism would be resisted by Redmond and the Nationalist party. Indeed, part of the problem that now arose from trying to reconcile the irreconcilable was the steady erosion of Redmond's (and by extension, the party's) authority among nationalists, as they were seen to give ground on the original 1912 proposals in order to placate the unionists and the British.

Although the bill did eventually complete its parliamentary course, by then the whole focus had shifted from parliament. In January 1913, just as the Home Rule bill was moving from the Commons to the Lords, the Ulster Volunteer Force was formed by the UUC. It was a local militia designed to resist the implementation of home rule when it passed into law. It had the support of leading Conservatives in England, many of whom sent cash. Top military men offered their assistance. The UVF soon comprised 100,000 men and drilled quite openly: drilling was legal only if approved by two magistrates and was conducted for a legal purpose. The magistrates were seldom a problem, being sympathetic, while the government turned a blind eye to the blatant illegality. The Conservative opposition was in effect giving its support to a treasonable conspiracy in support of the constitution.

The extent of the government's problem were seen in March 1914. Fearing that the UVF might raid arms depots, it instructed the commander-in-chief of the army in Ireland, General Paget, to prepare plans to frustrate any such attempt. Paget foolishly let it be known that officers with Ulster connections would not be obliged to take part in the action, but this merely prompted 56 other officers at the Curragh Military Camp in Co. Kildare to resign their commissions rather than move against Ulster. The shambles is sometimes called the Curragh Incident rather than the more traditional Curragh Mutiny, but the stronger term seems the fairer one, since the net effect was that the British government could no longer rely on the British army to act as an instrument of its will. For the first time since 1688, barrack-room politics had proved decisive.

In fact, the UVF had no need to raid arms depots, because in the following month they successfully landed 25,000 rifles and 1 million rounds of ammunition at three east Ulster ports, of which the Larne shipment was the biggest. The ease with which this was done and the fact that it was organised by the UUC, whose head was Edward Carson, a former solicitor-general of England, and whose principal organiser, James Craig, was a Conservative MP, demonstrated that unionism was prepared to stop at nothing in its defiance of parliament.

A last-ditch attempt to find some compromise between nationalist demands and unionist resistance came in July 1914, at the Buckingham Palace Conference, at which all parties were represented. But there was no magic formula. Irresistible force had met immovable object. There was no solution.

Then the Great War broke out. The Irish question was parked. Home Rule was enacted in September 1914 but with its provisions suspended until the war was over. By then, the whole world was changed and Ireland with it. Home rule was dead.

In November 1913, a group of advanced nationalists in Dublin formed the Irish Volunteers in conscious imitation of the UVF. The principal founder, Eoin Mac Néill, who had also founded the Gaelic League twenty years earlier, became its first commander-in-chief. Redmond was alarmed at the thought of a nationalist militia outside his control and quickly moved to tame it. He succeeded – or thought he had – by having his nominees take over the executive committee. But the Volunteers also proved of interest to the Fenians, who after many years of drift had been revived by Thomas J. Clarke, a veteran of the dynamite campaign of the 1880s who had served 15 years in prison. From now on it is best to use the Fenians' alternative name, the IRB (Irish Republican Brotherhood) because that was the term most commonly used by contemporaries.

Redmond's lack of real control was evident in the Howth gun-running of July 1914, when arms for the Irish Volunteers were landed in broad daylight at Howth, on the northern arm of Dublin Bay. This was a nationalist response to the Larne gun-running and, like it, was a publicity stunt. However, whereas

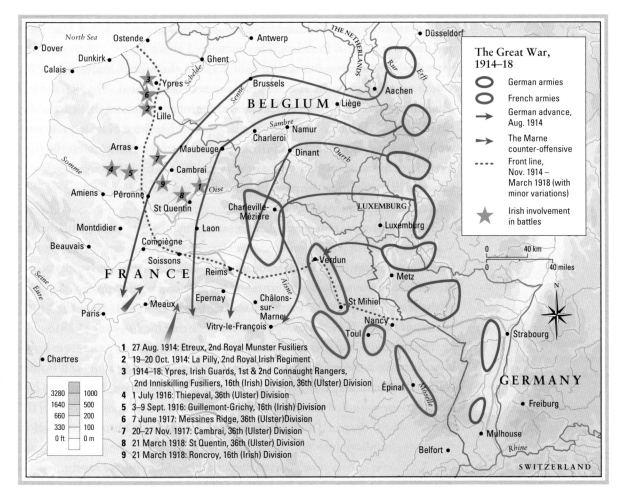

The Great War, 1914–18

German armies

French armies

German advance, Aug. 1914

The Marne counter-offensive

Front line, Nov. 1914 – March 1918 (with minor variations)

Irish involvement in battles

1   27 Aug. 1914: Etreux, 2nd Royal Munster Fusiliers
2   19–20 Oct. 1914: La Pilly, 2nd Royal Irish Regiment
3   1914–18: Ypres, Irish Guards, 1st & 2nd Connaught Rangers, 2nd Inniskilling Fusiliers, 16th (Irish) Division, 36th (Ulster) Division
4   1 July 1916: Thiepeval, 36th (Ulster) Division
5   3–9 Sept. 1916: Guillemont-Grichy, 16th (Irish) Division
6   7 June 1917: Messines Ridge, 36th (Ulster) Division
7   20–27 Nov. 1917: Cambrai, 36th (Ulster) Division
8   21 March 1918: St Quentin, 36th (Ulster) Division
9   21 March 1918: Roncroy, 16th (Irish) Division

Larne went off smoothly thanks to the collusion of the authorities, Howth ended in tragedy. Troops tried with little success to dispossess the Volunteers of their arms; the word of this failure spread, much to the merriment of the citizenry; and when a crowd of people in the city centre later taunted some British troops, things reached the point where the troops fired on the unarmed crowd, killing three of them. The contrast with Larne could hardly have been greater.

A month later, the outbreak of the Great War presented Redmond with a dilemma. Home rule was about to become law and now the United Kingdom, of which Ireland was and would remain a part under home rule, was at war. Redmond committed the Volunteers to the British war effort, thus splitting the movement. About 160,000 followed his call and re-constituted themselves as the National Volunteers. Many Irishmen went to fight on all fronts in the war. They fought honourably according to their lights and those of their political leaders. About 30,000 died. The survivors would return to a country transformed, one where their courage in the face of the Great War's horrors often counted for next to nothing.

Far Left: *James Larkin's statue in O'Connell Street, Dublin.*

Eamon de Valera.

Patrick Pearse.

chair and executed. The final coda came with hanging of Roger Casement in August on a charge of treason.

At first, public opinion was indifferent or hostile to the rising. Gradually, anger set in as the gruesome series of executions continued. The British made martyrs of the leaders. The novelist James Stephens, who kept a diary of Easter Week, noted contemporaneously: 'The truth is that Ireland is not cowed. She is excited a little. She was not with the revolution, but in a few months she will be, and her heart which was withering will be warmed by the knowledge that men thought her worth dying for.'

Stephens was right. The Easter Rising transformed Ireland. The British called it the Sinn Féin rebellion, although Sinn Féin had nothing to do with it. None the less, it was the Sinn Féin party which now became the focus of all those who celebrated the rising and were weary of Redmond. The party reconstituted itself in 1917. The founder, Arthur Griffith, stood aside to allow the leadership to pass to the most senior surviving garrison commander from the rising, Eamon de Valera.

The whole shape of Irish nationalism was changing. In part, it was a generational change. The leaders of the Nationalist party had all been young men in the 1880s. Now they seemed older than their years to a younger generation for whom the heroics of Easter Week were infinitely more glamorous than the parliamentary temporising of aging men. The Great War had blocked the emigration routes and bottled up a lot of young people in Ireland who might otherwise have found an outlet for their energies in the United States. For the new generation that had no personal memories of Parnell, Sinn Féin seemed fresh, vital and unapologetic.

Every political change, no matter how profound, requires a focus. The drift to Sinn Féin found its focus in the debate on conscription. Ireland was the only part of the United Kingdom in which conscription had not been imposed at the start of the war, an omission that spoke volumes in itself. The horrifying losses on the Somme in 1916 and at Passchendaele in 1917 tempted London to reconsider. At first, the prime minister, David Lloyd George, was not convinced of the effectiveness of extending conscription to Ireland, noting that it would produce relatively insignificant numbers of troops while robbing Irish agriculture – vital to the war effort – of labour. But continued losses forced the issue. In April 1918, the Military Services Act became law.

The Nationalists immediately withdrew from Westminster and returned to Ireland. There they made common cause with just about every element in

POBLACHT NA H EIREANN.

THE PROVISIONAL GOVERNMENT

OF THE

IRISH REPUBLIC

TO THE PEOPLE OF IRELAND.

IRISHMEN AND IRISHWOMEN : In the name of God and of the dead generations from which she receives her old tradition of nationhood, Ireland, through us, summons her children to her flag and strikes for her freedom.

Having organised and trained her manhood through her secret revolutionary organisation, the Irish Republican Brotherhood, and through her open military organisations, the Irish Volunteers and the Irish Citizen Army, having patiently perfected her discipline, having resolutely waited for the right moment to reveal itself, she now seizes that moment, and, supported by her exiled children in America and by gallant allies in Europe, but relying in the first on her own strength, she strikes in full confidence of victory.

We declare the right of the people of Ireland to the ownership of Ireland, and to the unfettered control of Irish destinies, to be sovereign and indefeasible. The long usurpation of that right by a foreign people and government has not extinguished the right, nor can it ever be extinguished except by the destruction of the Irish people. In every generation the Irish people have asserted their right to national freedom and sovereignty; six times during the past three hundred years they have asserted it in arms. Standing on that fundamental right and again asserting it in arms in the face of the world, we hereby proclaim the Irish Republic as a Sovereign Independent State, and we pledge our lives and the lives of our comrades-in-arms to the cause of its freedom, of its welfare, and of its exaltation among the nations.

The Irish Republic is entitled to, and hereby claims, the allegiance of every Irishman and Irishwoman. The Republic guarantees religious and civil liberty, equal rights and equal opportunities to all its citizens, and declares its resolve to pursue the happiness and prosperity of the whole nation and of all its parts, cherishing all the children of the nation equally, and oblivious of the differences carefully fostered by an alien government, which have divided a minority from the majority in the past.

Until our arms have brought the opportune moment for the establishment of a permanent National Government, representative of the whole people of Ireland and elected by the suffrages of all her men and women, the Provisional Government, hereby constituted, will administer the civil and military affairs of the Republic in trust for the people.

We place the cause of the Irish Republic under the protection of the Most High God, Whose blessing we invoke upon our arms, and we pray that no one who serves that cause will dishonour it by cowardice, inhumanity, or rapine. In this supreme hour the Irish nation must, by its valour and discipline and by the readiness of its children to sacrifice themselves for the common good, prove itself worthy of the august destiny to which it is called.

Signed on Behalf of the Provisional Government,

THOMAS J. CLARKE.

SEAN Mac DIARMADA, THOMAS MacDONAGH,
P. H. PEARSE, EAMONN CEANNT,
JAMES CONNOLLY. JOSEPH PLUNKETT.

Part of Sackville Street (now O'Connell Street) after the Rising.

nationalist civil society in opposition to conscription. It left the party in an awkward position, for it was implicitly conceding Sinn Féin's point that Westminster was a waste of time. If nationalist voters were asked to support abstention, why not vote for the real abstentionists?

The key to the success of the anti-conscription campaign was the unambiguous manner in which it united all shades of nationalism, especially – and most importantly – the Catholic church. A pledge to oppose conscription was signed by nearly two million people throughout the country on 21 April: it had been drafted by Eamon de Valera, the Sinn Féin leader. There was a general strike on the 23rd. There were demonstrations. It became clear to the government that any attempt to enforce the conscription law would result in massive civil disobedience and violence. Instead it funked the issue. By the time the war ended in November, conscription was a dead letter.

Conscription destroyed the Nationalist party. It had a fight on its hands with Sinn Féin up to that point, but it had not done too badly. True, it had lost three by-elections to the younger party in 1917 and early 1918, most famously in Clare where de Valera took Daniel O'Connell's old seat to launch a political career that would lead him to dominate his country at the mid-century. But as late as February 1918, the Nationalists had held South Armagh in a by-election against a strong Sinn Féin candidate and when John Redmond died in March, his seat in Waterford was held for the party by his son. In April, just two weeks before the introduction of conscription, the party held its seat in the East Tyrone by-election. There were special circumstances in all three Nationalist victories: the party was better organised in Ulster than elsewhere and in better shape to fight elections. In Waterford, there was a large sympathy vote.

Once conscription became the burning issue, however, the old party was doomed. When the war ended, Lloyd George called a general election for December 1918. Sinn Féin annihilated the Home Rulers to become the undisputed voice of nationalist Ireland. Pledged not to take their seats at Westminster, they constituted themselves as Dáil Eireann, the assembly of Ireland, meeting for the first time on 21 January 1919. On the same day, two unarmed policemen were shot dead in an ambush in Co. Tipperary in what was the first action of the Irish war of independence.

This war was prosecuted by the Irish Republican Army (IRA), as the Volunteers now styled themselves. Their relationship to Sinn Féin was ambiguous, although sharing a common separatist sensibility. There was no sense in which they were firmly under civilian control and direction, although this was advanced as a useful fiction. The war of independence was a series of sporadic regional guerrilla conflicts, depending on the initiative of vigorous and committed local commanders. It was an ambush war, directed in the first place at the isolated barracks of the Royal Irish Constabulary. By forcing the RIC from large parts of the countryside, the IRA weakened the local eyes and ears of British rule in rural Ireland.

James Connolly.

The British responded with a mixture of regular troops and auxiliaries, the infamous Black and Tans. It was a dirty war. The Black and Tans were ill-disciplined and often drunk. Many were rootless veterans of the western front, brutalised by their experiences. They were terrifying when they ran amok, as they did in Cork city centre and in the little town of Balbriggan, just north of Dublin, both of which they burned to the ground. The IRA had a number of successful ambush battles against crown troops, especially in Co. Cork: the actions at Crossbarry and Kilmichael were particularly celebrated. Equally, however, the Cork campaign took a sectarian turn and a number of atrocities were committed against local Protestants. The new republic carried some antique baggage.

The military campaign was paralleled by a civil one. Sinn Féin established the rudiments of an alternative civil administration to the British, complete with a department of finance to raise loans, a very successful alternative court system to adjudicate local disputes and a vigorous propaganda arm. The key figure was Michael Collins.

Not yet 30, this extraordinary force of nature was simultaneously Minister of Finance in the alternative administration, where he successfully administered the raising of Dáil loans both in Ireland and the United States, and director of intelligence of the IRA, in which role he ruthlessly infiltrated and damaged the British security system in Dublin Castle. Collins was prepared to play very dirty indeed, as he showed on the morning of Bloody Sunday, 21 November 1920, when his men executed eleven British agents in their beds in cold blood. In retaliation, a party of Auxiliaries killed twelve people in Croke

Members of the First Dáil on 21 January 1919.

Park, the Dublin headquarters of the GAA, when they fired into the crowd during a football game that afternoon.

The war was fought to a stalemate by the summer of 1921. By then, the island had been partitioned. The Government of Ireland Act 1920 – successor to the ill-fated Home Rule Act of 1914 that never saw the light of day – bowed to the inevitable. Ulster could not be coerced into a nationalist state. So the 1920 act created two parliaments, one for the six most Protestant counties of Ulster, and one for the rest of the country. The northern parliament began to function and lasted until 1972. The southern parliament was stillborn, bypassed by the Dáil.

The birth of Northern Ireland was accompanied by an orgy of sectarian violence in the years 1920–22. The war of independence spread north and became entangled with the trauma of partition. The IRA attacked police and army as in the south; Protestant mobs drove Catholic workers from the Belfast shipyards; the IRA retaliated by burning businesses and big houses in rural Ulster to try to take the pressure off their beleaguered co-religionists in Belfast; the UVF was re-formed as the Ulster Special Constabulary – the notorious B Specials – a viciously partisan Protestant militia; sixty-one people died in Belfast alone in the single month of March 1922.

In essence, the sectarian civil war that had been postponed by the outbreak of the Great War had now broken out in the Ulster cockpit. Inevitably, given the local superiority of Protestant numbers and the fact that they now controlled the levers of the state, the Protestants were able to brings a greater terror to bear than the Catholics. There were atrocities committed on both sides: it was not all one-way traffic. But the Protestant traffic was more lethal. Moreover, it polluted its own community, as well as terrorising the Catholic one, by permitting the agents of the newly partitioned statelet literally to get away with murder.

The IRA's war of independence ended with a truce in July 1921. Negotiations between the Sinn Fèin leadership and the British began in October and culminated in a treaty proposal on 6 December. It gave southern Ireland effective independence, along the same lines as Canada, but retained the oath of allegiance to the crown and therefore stopped short of a republic. The principal Irish negotiators were Griffith and Collins. De Valera, the political leader of Irish nationalism and the most subtle negotiating intellect, stayed at home. This was ostensibly to prepare the people for the inevitable compromise solution to come.

Michael Collins.

Which made it all the more surprising that de Valera himself was one of the first to repudiate the terms of the treaty. After the heady five years of republican expectation since the rising, there was bound to be some degree of disappointment. None the less, the Dáil approved the treaty by a narrow margin. There followed an uneasy few months before dissidents in the IRA occupied the Four Courts in Dublin. Collins, by now chairman of the provisional government in charge of Ireland until the terms of the Irish Free State set up by the treaty could take over, was pressurised by the British into rooting them out. This he did, in June 1922, using field guns.

This action tripped off the civil war. It was bitter, as all these things are, but the government held all the big cards. There was little resistance outside Munster and by April 1923 it was over. But it claimed the lives of Griffith – from a stroke – and Collins, from a sniper's bullet in his native Co. Cork. In the meantime, the Irish Free State had been born in December 1922. The last British troops left, as did the last British officials. The union flag came down and the tricolour flag first introduced by the Young Irelanders 74 years earlier now flew on all public buildings.

There were now two states in Ireland. In the south, the Irish Free State was effectively an independent country. It was overwhelmingly Catholic. In the six counties of the north east, Northern Ireland was an autonomous province within the United Kingdom. It had a population that was roughly two-thirds Protestant, but with a Catholic minority inflexibly opposed to the very existence of the state.

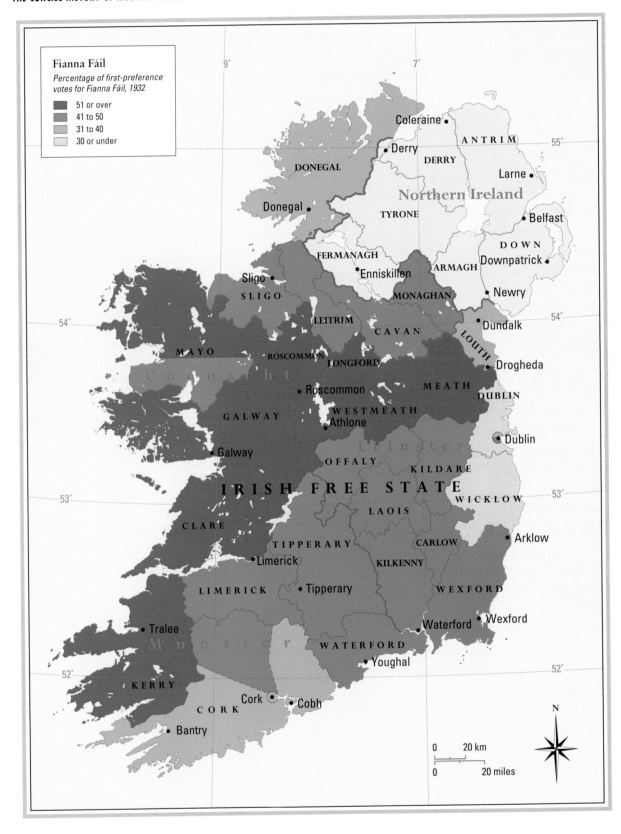

Fianna Fáil
*Percentage of first-preference
votes for Fianna Fáil, 1932*

51 or over
41 to 50
31 to 40
30 or under

CHAPTER 10

TWO STATES
One Island, Two States
1923–60

After the end of the civil war, the Irish Free State got down to business. Its governing party, Cumann na nGaedheal, comprised those in Sinn Féin who supported the treaty settlement. Its leader, now that Griffith and Collins were dead, was W. T. Cosgrave, an uncharismatic man who had fought in 1916. The dominant figure in the first five years of the government was the brilliant but authoritarian Kevin O'Higgins, the Minister for Home Affairs. Eoin Mac Néill was Minister for Education. Four other ministers had, like Cosgrave, fought in 1916.

The opposition – the political opponents of the treaty – retained the name Sinn Féin. They refused to take their seats in the Dáil and remained outside formal politics until 1927. In effect, this gave the Cumann na nGaedheal a clear parliamentary run. They could concentrate on government and neglect politics.

W. T. Cosgrave, leader of the Irish Free State from 1922 to 1932.

The principal achievement of Cosgrave's government during its ten years in office was the establishment of the institutions of the new state. It fought the civil war ruthlessly to a definitive conclusion. In the midst of that war, it established the police force of the new state – the Garda Siochana (Guardians of the Peace) – as an unarmed body. This was a remarkable change from British days. Henceforth, policing was to be consensual rather than coercive. The success of this courageous initiative underlined the basic legitimacy of the new state, even in the immediate aftermath of the civil war. There is no doubt that a majority of people in the Free State accepted the treaty settlement, although with varying degrees of enthusiasm.

Economically, the Free State was orthodox and conservative, reflecting its dependence on the powerful civil servants who headed the Department of Finance. The one major economic initiative undertaken by the government was

the establishment in 1927 of the Electricity Supply Board and the building of a big hydro-electric generating station on the River Shannon at Ardnacrusha, near Limerick. This was a departure from economic orthodoxy, which was otherwise all pervasive. It established what was a nationalised company in all but name as a monopoly supplier of electricity throughout the state.

A boundary commission established under the terms of the treaty produced no change in the border. This failure – dashing the confident expectations of many nationalists in both north and south – reduced the government's prestige and ended the political career of the hapless Eoin Mac Néill, who had been the Free State's representative on the commission.

Cumann na nGaedheal consciously embraced the support of members of the old southern unionist establishment, which further compromised them in the eyes of their opponents. They also drew the remnants of the Redmondite tradition to themselves. They were consciously the creators and guardians of the institutions of the state, but in pursuing this obsession with institutions they neglected the sinews of ordinary politics.

None of this mattered until 1926, because there was no substantial opposition to Cumann na nGaedheal. But in that year Eamon de Valera failed to persuade Sinn Féin to abandon its policy of abstention if the oath of allegiance were to be removed. He immediately left Sinn Féin and established Fianna Fáil (the soldiers of destiny). Still abstentionist, the new party gave notice of its potential by winning 26 per cent of the poll and 44 seats in the general election of June 1927.

The next month, the government's best intellect and most commanding personality, Kevin O'Higgins, was murdered by IRA dissidents. He had never been forgiven for being the hard man in the civil war cabinet. His death moved the government to propose a bill obliging all Dáil candidates to swear that they would take the oath of allegiance if elected. This presented de Valera with an acute dilemma. Fianna Fáil deputies would have to take the hated oath or face the same sterile future as Sinn Féin. The whole logic of the break with Sinn Féin pointed towards the need to cut this Gordian knot. Accordingly, de Valera wrestled with his conscience and won – not for the first or last time – declaring the oath to be a mere 'empty formula', a curious conclusion in view of the fact that it had seemed worth a civil war just five years earlier.

Cosgrave called a snap election in September. This saw the Fianna Fáil vote increase to 35 per cent and their seat count to 57. Sinn Féin was wiped out as a political force. Fianna Fáil was now clearly the standard bearer of the republican anti-treatyites.

De Valera came to power in 1932. His Fianna Fáil party was pledged to fight vigorously against partition and for the reunification of the country; for the

Ardnacrusha Hydro-electric works near Limerick.

revival of the Irish language; for the dismantling of the constitutional arrangements laid down in the treaty; for the break-up of large ranches and the creation of the greatest possible number of small family farms; and for the abandonment of Cumann na nGaedheal's free trade policies in favour of protection and the development of native industry behind tariff barriers.

On the first two policies, Fianna Fáil failed dismally. No Irish nationalist of any kind had a clue what to do about Northern Ireland, except to hurl invective at Ulster unionists. On the language issue, it seemed that the Irish people were as utilitarian as Daniel O'Connell had been a century earlier. The whole propaganda apparatus of the state was directed to the promotion of the language. To no avail: the decline continued inexorably. Irish people voted with their tongues.

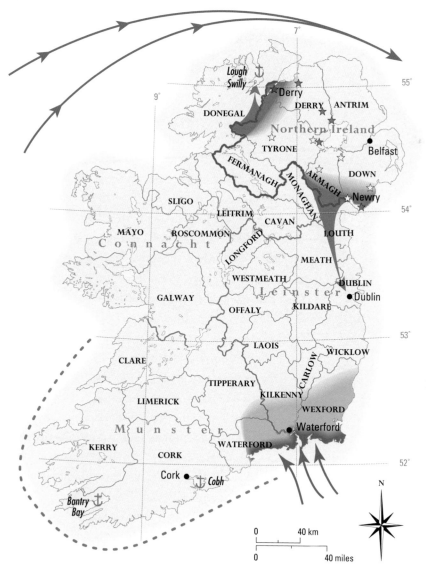

Far Left: *Eamon De Valera.*

On the constitutional front, de Valera was in his element. Half Machiavelli, half sententious Jesuit, he did not hesitate. The crown's representative in the Free State, the governor-general, was effectively fired and replaced by a de Valera crony who barely appeared in public and who by his reticence made a deliberate laughing stock of the office. He abolished the oath of allegiance by legislation in 1933, to the fury of the British. He enacted a new constitution in 1937, replacing that established under the treaty. It was republican in all but name. The governor-general was replaced by a president; a formal territorial claim was made to Northern Ireland; and the 'special position' of the Catholic church was formally recognised.

Like Parnell before him, the old Fenian de Valera was making his accommodation with the Church. In fact, he was a man of exemplary orthodoxy in religious matters. One of his principal advisers on the constitution was John Charles McQuaid, a cleric of powerful if narrow intellect, soon to be archbishop of Dublin and the dominant figure in the Catholic Church at the mid century. De Valera occupied the mainstream of Irish nationalist life in which the Church was the supreme arbiter of moral value. Ireland was a country saturated in Catholicism: the unspoken assumption was that the basic integrating force in society was the shared Catholicism of its citizens. Even the GAA, with all its Fenian inheritance, was full of priests. In this context, de Valera's piety was unremarkable. It was perfectly natural that he should express the common moral values of his community.

The ease with which Fianna Fáil had taken over the state apparatus, had amended it in fulfilment of its election promises and had reached a modus vivendi with a civil service which it had previously held in suspicion indicated the extent to which a stable political consensus had been established. Fianna Fáil was the party of the nation, a populist people's party with broad cross-class appeal in the classic tradition of Irish political mobilisation. Cumann na nGaedheal reacted badly to its loss of office, flirting briefly with a neo-fascist group called the Blueshirts before reinventing itself as Fine Gael. It remained pre-eminently the party of the state, emphasising institutions rather than people; less ruthless about organisation; more high-minded about policy; often wanting for the common touch and appealing disproportionately to large farmers and the upper middle class. Fianna Fáil leaned to the left; Fine Gael was very firmly on the right.

What both parties had was a basic commitment to democracy and the rule of law. There were anti-democratic elements close to both: Fianna Fáil was still

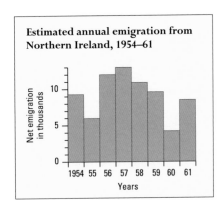

Estimated annual emigration from Northern Ireland, 1954–61

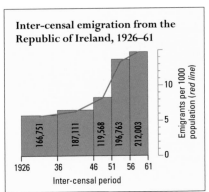

Inter-censal emigration from the Republic of Ireland, 1926–61

indulgent towards the IRA while, as noted above, Fine Gael emerged from an entanglement with the Blueshirts, an organisation of overheated Catholic zealots in search of an Hibernian Mussolini: all they got was an ex-chief of police called O'Duffy. But the remarkable aspect of Ireland in the 1930s was the extent to which fashionable anti-democratic movements failed to gain ground.

On the economic front, the promise to develop Irish industry behind tariff barriers was redeemed under the direction of the energetic young Minister for Industry & Commerce, Sean Lemass. The necessary legislation was put in place by the mid 1930s and an experiment in economic self-sufficiency began which would last for a quarter of a century. Fianna Fáil were much more energetic about establishing public enterprises such as the national airline, Aer Lingus, which was founded in 1936.

On the social side, the new government displayed considerable energy in slum clearance and the provision of new suburban public housing. But the crunch came in the countryside, because there was one more election promise to honour which caused a major crisis. De Valera had promised to withhold the annuities due to the British Treasury in repayment of loans extended to tenants under the various land purchase acts, of which Wyndham's Act of 1903 was the best known. He did so. The British retaliated by slapping import duties on Irish produce, of which cattle were the most important. This so-called 'economic war' dragged on until 1938, causing much hardship in an Ireland already feeling the effects of the depression that followed the Wall Street Crash of 1929.

The economic war was finally settled under the terms of the Anglo-Irish agreement of 1938, which also tackled other irritants in Anglo-Irish relations. The annuities were converted into a single lump sum which Dublin paid to London. On the constitutional side, there was much clearing of the air, as the British reconciled themselves to de Valera's neo-republican constitution of 1937. De Valera also secured the return of three ports which the Royal Navy had retained under the terms of the treaty.

When World War II broke out, Dublin demonstrated its independence in the most emphatic way by remaining neutral. In this, it simply did what every other

Death Rate for Tuberculosis, 1950–54

- Increase
- Decrease up to 30%
- Decrease from 31 to 60%
- Decrease over 60%

Subject to U.K. National Health organisation founded 1946

DONEGAL

SLIGO
LEITRIM CAVAN MONAGHAN LOUTH
MAYO ROSCOMMON LONGFORD
MEATH
WESTMEATH
GALWAY DUBLIN
OFFALY KILDARE
LAOIS WICKLOW
CLARE
CARLOW
TIPPERARY KILKENNY
LIMERICK WEXFORD

KERRY WATERFORD
CORK

N

0   40 km
0   40 miles

small nation in Europe did if it could get away with it. Public opinion was overwhelmingly for neutrality, although this did not stop significant numbers of volunteers from the south joining the British forces. Nor did it stop elements in the IRA from trying to cosy up to Nazi Germany.

Officially, de Valera maintained a policy of the most scrupulous neutrality. Unofficially, Ireland was neutral for Britain. Whether out of prudence or conviction, the government showed 'a certain consideration for Britain'. Thus, German airmen shot down over Ireland were promptly interned for the duration of the war. British (or other allied) pilots were slipped across the border into Northern Ireland and no questions asked.

The combination of economic isolation caused by the tariff regime, the inevitable shortages caused by the war, Ireland's geographical remoteness and its aloofness from a conflict that was convulsing the world was enervating. The fizz went out of the government. The reforming impulse that had made the 1930s exciting weakened. The war ended. Europe, boosted by Marshall Aid, produced an astonishing economic recovery in the 1950s in which Ireland did not share. The country was still run for the benefit of a deeply conservative farming class. In effect, the land settlement and the absence of heavy industry had ensured that Ireland's political revolution would be socially conservative.

De Valera was a romantic reactionary. He believed in the moral superiority of the small family farm, of simple rural life over urban life, of an Ireland living as far as possible in seclusion from the world and steering her own course. The net effect of all this was that the Republic of Ireland (the Republic had formally been declared in 1949) was the only country in the capitalist world whose economy actually contracted in the post-war years. The population of the state declined in the first forty years of independence. By the late '50s, the game was up for social and economic self-sufficiency. This old ideal, which went back to Arthur Griffith's Sinn Féin, had brought the country to its knees.

Apart from de Valera's social vision, one reason why the Republic pursued these policies long after they had anything to offer was that they suited the country's collective self-image. Like many ethnic nationalisms across Europe, there was a distinct anti-modern side to Irish independence. The imperial master represented an oppressive modernism; freedom meant a retreat into a simpler, more moral order. De Valera's vision of domestic frugality and simplicity was reflected in popular attitudes. The rural small holder was regarded as the ideal national type. In many European countries, this kind of sensibility produced fascist movements of one sort or another; in Ireland, at least spared that, it eventually produced a grand stasis.

De Valera was Taoiseach (as the prime minister was called under the 1937 constitution) for all but six years from 1932 to 1959. He dominated Irish life precisely because he embodied the aspirations and ideals of the population. He was tall, austere, commanding. To his political followers, he was simply 'The Chief'. To his enemies he was, in Oliver St John Gogarty's memorable phrase, 'the Spanish onion in the Irish stew'. But no one could deny his command of public opinion, his devious and serpentine intellect, his sincere passion for the Irish language and the republican ideals of the old Sinn Féin. Sadly, he overstayed his welcome by at least ten years.

One other group was entirely pleased with the introverted Ireland of the de Valera years. The Catholic Church liked the idea of Ireland as a kind of spiritual *cordon sanitaire* from which the excesses of secular modernity were excluded. The ultramontane church bequeathed by Cardinal Cullen in the nineteenth century was authoritarian, dogmatic and – by 1950 or so – at the height of its influence and prestige. Its moral writ ran with irresistible force.

When the coalition government of 1948–51 – the first non-de Valera administration since 1932 – tried to introduce free medical care for mothers and children under 16, it sparked off a church-state clash which the church won hands down. The sponsoring minister, a left-wing maverick named Noel Browne, was forced to resign. Members of the cabinet wrote to John Charles McQuaid, the archbishop of Dublin and principal opponent of the scheme, in the most fawning and obsequious terms to prove their loyalty. McQuaid's objection was that Catholic social teaching decreed that such services as Browne proposed were the province of the family rather than the state.

It was quite a thing to be a Catholic bishop in Ireland in the mid-twentieth century. It was a guarantee of immense deference and prestige. Catholic Ireland, it seemed, was the last vibrant corner of the Victorian world. Religious observance and devotion were nearly universal. Almost every Catholic went to Mass each Sunday; abstention was a social scandal. There were sodalities, public processions, devotions such as benediction and the forty hours, missions and retreats, and an overwhelming Marian devotion. There were priests everywhere. Churches were full to overflowing. Catholic pamphlets and tracts and devotional books sold strongly. There was little or no public criticism of the Church or any tradition of anti-clericalism. It was said by some that the people were not priest-ridden, rather the priests were people-ridden, so ubiquitous was the spirit of submissive orthodoxy.

Relations with Protestants were cool to frigid. Ecumenism was for the future. For the moment, the Church insisted on the primacy of its teaching and held all other Christian groups to be in varying degrees of error. This was not a church that encouraged theological speculation or internal debate.

The Irish Catholic Church also had an enormous missionary presence overseas. In every part of the English-speaking world and in most of Africa, Irish priests, nuns and brothers were to be found. By the middle of the century, there were more than 10,000 Irish missionaries scattered around the world, not counting priests of Irish birth who chose to serve overseas. It was an impressive statistic for a country so sparsely populated. The Irish church regarded its missionary outreach as a spiritual analogue to Britain's material empire and all the more honourable for that. The Irish missionaries did not simply spread the faith; they provided teachers and medical personnel in huge numbers.

At home, the entire education system was denominational – this key ambition of the church had been fulfilled promptly in the 1920s on securing independence. The schools were run by priests, nuns and brothers. The latter, in particular, educated generations of lower-middle class boys who might otherwise have received little or no schooling at all. Still, it was a utilitarian, Gradgrind type of education for the most part – another Victorian survival. And behind the benign and selfless achievements of generations of clerical teachers lay the dark secret of sexual abuse of minors, in schools, orphanages and penal institutions run for the state by religious orders.

The traditional church was obsessed with sex and the sins of the flesh. These were, in a sense, the only real sins. The deep puritanism of the church was partly a further manifestation of an antique world in which Victorian values persisted long after they had been subverted elsewhere. But it was also a psychological prop in the whole post-Famine settlement. The need for marriages to be delayed until farms could be inherited; the wretched celibacy of many who had nothing to inherit and therefore nothing to offer a spouse; the extraordinary prestige in which celibate clergy were held: these were social inventions, designed to stabilise rural society in the post-Famine period. Irish society got the morality it needed. In this as in much else, church and people were one.

This unity of sentiment found many forms of expression. Few were more damaging to the country's international reputation than the ferocious literary censorship. It was put in place in 1929 and lasted until 1967. During that time nearly all contemporary Irish writers suffered at its hands, as well as an impressive representation of modern masters. The original legislation had arisen from the report of a Committee on Evil Literature, a body whose very name suggested a begging of the question rather than an examination of it. Interestingly, the theatre was excluded from the Censorship Board's remit, so that there was no institution in independent Ireland equivalent to the Lord Chamberlain in the UK. In this one particular, Ireland was formally more liberal than Britain. Even there, however, the censoring impulse was seldom absent: there were *causes célèbres* at regular intervals.

In 1926, in a re-run of the Playboy riots of 1907, Sean O'Casey's *Plough and*

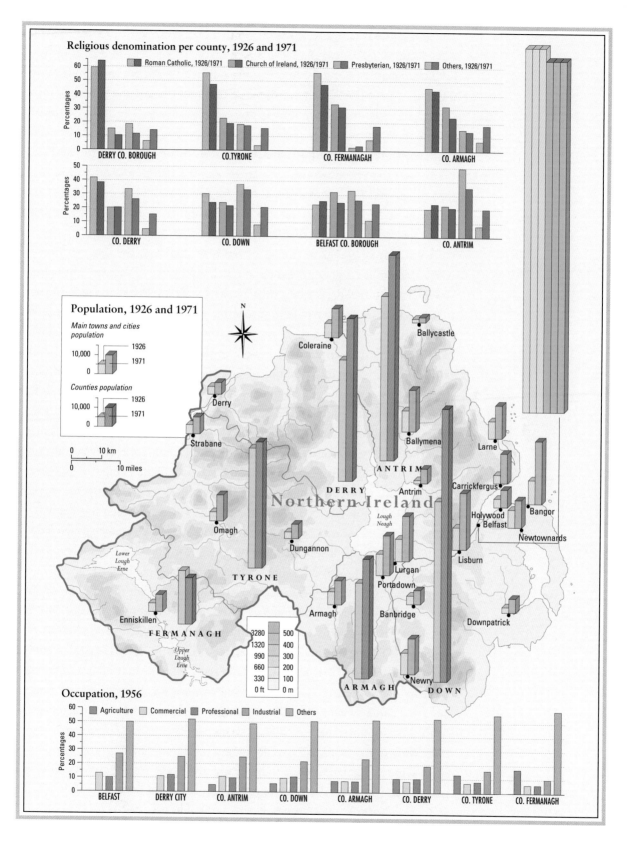

Religious denomination per county, 1926 and 1971

Roman Catholic, 1926/1971   Church of Ireland, 1926/1971   Presbyterian, 1926/1971   Others, 1926/1971

Percentages

DERRY CO. BOROUGH   CO. TYRONE   CO. FERMANAGAH   CO. ARMAGH

CO. DERRY   CO. DOWN   BELFAST CO. BOROUGH   CO. ANTRIM

Population, 1926 and 1971

Main towns and cities population

10,000   1926
                1971
0

Counties population

10,000   1926
                1971
0

N

Coleraine   Ballycastle

Derry

Strabane   Ballymena   Larne

Carrickfergus

0   10 km
0   10 miles

Omagh   Antrim   Holywood   Bangor
                     Antrim   Belfast
Dungannon   Newtownards

Lower Lough Erne   Lisburn

Lurgan

TYRONE   Portadown

Enniskillen   Armagh   Banbridge

FERMANAGH   Downpatrick

Upper Lough Erne   3280   500
                                1320   400
                                990   300
                                660   200
                                330   100
                                0 ft   0 m

Newry

ARMAGH   DOWN

Occupation, 1956

Agriculture   Commercial   Professional   Industrial   Others

Percentages

BELFAST   DERRY CITY   CO. ANTRIM   CO. DOWN   CO. ARMAGH   CO. DERRY   CO. TYRONE   CO. FERMANAGH

DERRY   Northern Ireland   Lough Neagh

the Stars caused a riot in the Abbey by offending nationalist pieties. Following the rejection of his next play, *The Silver Tassie*, by the Abbey board, O'Casey left for England, never to return. He was a difficult man, but the stifling atmosphere of a country content with censorship and demanding placebos rather than challenges in the theatre was no incentive to stay. The Abbey entered a period of prolonged decline and mediocrity, despite the presence of talented individuals in its company. Its managing director from 1941 to 1967 was Ernest Blythe, who had been Minister for Finance in the 1920s and had famously cut the old-age pension in order to balance the new state's books. Blythe was narrow-minded and cocksure, and his period in office is generally held to have been an extended nadir in the theatre's fortunes.

It was one of the great ironies of the new state that the one art form for which Ireland had a genuinely international reputation – literature in English – should have suffered so grievously at the hands of the new establishment. Ireland had a very sparse inheritance in fine art, in architecture whether public or domestic (and much of that heritage, in the form of fine country houses, had been gleefully torched in the Troubles), in public sculpture, in classical music (although rich in the folk tradition), in dance or in most of the higher arts. Its achievements in international scholarship were modest. But in literature, it had a world reputation and deserved it. At the foundation of the state, Yeats, Joyce, Shaw and O'Casey were all alive. Synge was not long dead. An Anglo-Irish tradition running back from Wilde to Farquhar and Congreve had been constantly renewed. Flann O'Brien, Patrick Kavanagh, Brendan Behan and other writers of international distinction would emerge in the bleak censorship years. Beckett was in Paris. Louis MacNeice was in London. The astonishing productivity of Irish writers seemed endlessly self-renewing, yet their own country treated them as an enemy within. It was the ultimate revenge of the Abbey rioters on Yeats's naive idealism. The peasant republic was aesthetically challenged.

The securing of independence did nothing to staunch the flow of emigration. The population of Ireland had fallen in every decennial census since the Famine until the departure of the British from the Twenty-Six counties that became the Free State and later the Republic. The population remained almost static from 1926 to 1951. However, that alone indicated that natural increase – in a country where large families were the norm – was insufficient to compensate for death and departure. The 1950s, however, brought a demographic collapse. It is estimated that over 400,000 Irish people emigrated between 1951 and 1961, this from a population of less than 3 million! This haemorrhage, combined with rates of infant mortality above the norm for the developed world and the scourge of TB among young people, offset the exceptionally high rate of marital fertility in the period. The Irish families who stayed or survived were very large by international standards, but not enough stayed or survived.

The 1950s brought the Republic firmly up against the reality that it had been pursuing an economic policy of protectionism and autarky which was leading it to disaster. At independence, Ireland had been modestly prosperous in comparison with most of north-west Europe and richer on any measure than many other new post-imperial nations in the old Habsburg lands, not to mention the Balkans or most of the Iberian peninsula. In one critical respect, it had an overwhelming comparative advantage: literacy levels stood at close to 100 per cent. The comparable figure in Poland was 70 per cent. Ireland was not rich, but it certainly was not poor. Yet within thirty years of independence, by the 1950s, the country was in crisis. In that decade, not only was there a terrifying rate of emigration, Ireland's economy grew at only one-fifth of the average rate for Western Europe. Between 1955 and 1957, the total volume of goods and services consumed in Ireland fell. All this happened in the middle of one of the biggest international capitalist booms in history, fuelled in Europe by Marshall Aid.

Whatever case there had been for the establishment of a tariff regime in the 1930s – there had been an economic case made out, and Ireland was not the only young country then or since to try to build up its economy behind tariff barriers – there was none now. In fact, the economic case for protection had been a smoke screen. Behind it all lay an ideology, a conscious turning away from the world of vulgar modernity represented by the old imperial master: 'pagan England'. The astonishing deference shown to church leaders; the willing acceptance of censorship; the embracing of wartime neutrality; the GAA's ban on its players playing or even attending scheduled 'foreign games': all proceeded from a common sensibility. At its root was a determination to discover uniquely Irish answers, to insist on the autonomy of the Irish mind. It was a nice idea, but it had nothing to do with economics and it nearly wrecked the country.

Northern Ireland too enjoyed a long sleep from the 1920s to the '60s. The one part of Ireland that had fought most bitterly against home rule was the only part to get it. The province's devolved government was established to suit the convenience of the local Protestant unionist majority and nobody else. The IRA had done its best to strangle Northern Ireland at birth. The new state was born on the back of a military victory for the unionists in 1922. Nationalists were to be a despised enemy in the eyes of their new rulers.

Ulster unionists created a state in their own image and for their own community. From the first, Northern Ireland was obsessed with community security. The police were augmented by the Ulster Special Constabulary (the B Specials), an armed local militia, who were effectively the UVF in another guise. Many were Great War veterans. Few were squeamish about violence, a lack of scruple which was in fairness reciprocated by the IRA. The police and the USC had at their backs the Special Powers Act, originally enacted in 1922 at the height of the IRA war to give the state emergency powers. It was not repealed until 1973. In effect, it gave the Minister of Home Affairs power to rule by decree. In its indifference to civil liberties and the normal constitutional checks and balances, it was unique in the western world.

Northern Ireland was financially beholden to London and unable to formulate any economic policy to deal with the damage done to the local economy in the aftermath of the Wall Street crash. Things were so bad in the early 1930s that the unemployed briefly threw aside their sectarian animosities to form a united front. This moment did not last and 1935 saw the worst sectarian rioting in Belfast since 1922.

World War II brought a temporary revival, as the economy went on a war footing and unemployment was almost eliminated. There was also a generational change in unionism. Craig died in 1940 and was succeeded, not by one of the next generation, but by his near contemporary John Miller Andrews. He retained Craig's old guard, but a party revolt in 1943 brought the younger and more energetic Basil Brooke (later to become Lord Brookeborough) to power. This change at the top did not signify any liberalising of sectarian attitudes. Even the shared privations of the war – Belfast was bombed heavily by the Luftwaffe in 1941 and hundreds died – did nothing to lessen communal divisions or the essentially sectarian nature of the partition.

Both sides were caught in a trap with nowhere to go. Unionist gain could only mean nationalist loss and vice versa. The logic of the nationalist position was as bleak. Unable to challenge the existence of the state and incapable of recognising its legitimacy, its politics were condemned to futility. In local government, where there might be a nationalist majority, unionists ensured their continued dominance through a shameless policy of gerrymandering. Derry was the most notable, but not the only, example of this.

The establishment of the British welfare state after World War II disturbed this pattern. The benefits of the new system – combined with those of the British educational reforms which effectively opened up secondary schooling to all regardless of income – were applied indiscriminately. Some unionist ultras resented this rewarding of treachery, and indeed it was to have devastating consequences for unionism in the late 1960s.

From 1956 to 1962 the IRA conducted a sporadic campaign of bombings, arms raids and ambushes along the border. It was a sad coda to this whole period. It was a half-hearted effort which seemed to symbolise the enervated state of militant republicanism. There were many minor actions, but most were contained in west Ulster. There was no mass mobilisation of nationalists. Belfast was almost untouched. Brookeborough introduced internment and locked up

Sean MacBride (c. 1950), son of one of the executed leaders of the 1916 Rising. He was a lawyer, ex-Chief of Staff of the IRA, Minister for External Affairs 1948–51, founder of Amnesty International, the only person ever to win the Nobel and Lenin Peace prizes.

as many militants as he could find. Interestingly, de Valera did the same in the Republic: no one was going to out-republican him. In all, twelve IRA men and six policemen died in the border campaign. It was such small beer compared to what was to come.

De Valera retired in 1959, Brookeborough in 1963. The 1960s was to prove the most tumultuous decade since partition on both sides of the border.

In the Republic, it heralded a genuinely new era. The old protectionist policies were abandoned. Free trade and inward investment were embraced. There was a thorough going intellectual spring clean in the corridors of power: much of the new thinking came from the upper reaches of the civil service. Lemass's eventual succession in 1959, after de Valera finally stood aside, was crucial. He showed remarkable political skill and courage in dismantling the series of eco-

Sean Lemass. He held the portfolio of Industry and Commerce from 1932 until 1959 with three short breaks. He was responsible for the policy of protection in the 1930s and for dismantling it in favour of free trade in the 1960s, when he finally succeeded de Valera as Taoiseach.

CHAPTER 11

IRELAND SINCE THE 1960s
Troubles, Booms and Busts 1960–2005

It had been said of Sinn Féin and the other nationalists who had made the revolution of 1918–22 that they were the most conservative revolutionaries in history. It is hard to argue with this assessment. The overwhelming sense one has of the new Irish state from the 1920s to the 1950s was of an entrenched conservatism. This expressed itself in a number of ways. There was an insistent emphasis on the institutional stability of the state. The Westminster model of politics was not challenged: it simply migrated from the Thames to Leinster House. The new social and political establishment was economically sclerotic. The Irish economy was based on farming, and the farmers had had their real revolution in 1903, when Wyndham's Land Act had established them as proprietors on farms many of which were not, and never would be, economically viable. The Irish economy was not so much undynamic as anti-dynamic. This induced a profound conservatism among property holders, both on the land itself and among their cousins who manned the civil service and provided the teachers. One historian has spoken of the triumph of the 'possessor principle' in this period: in a static economy, it pays to hold what you have. It pays to see economic and commercial activity as a zero-sum game, a form of beggar my neighbour. And so it was.

All this was compounded – indeed endorsed – by the Catholic Church in its hour of hubristic triumph. The same farmers and civil servants and teachers who were at the heart of the new nationalist consensus gave their sons and daughters to the church in extraordinary numbers. The Irish Catholic church was still the ultramontane juggernaut that Paul Cullen had created in the nineteenth century, emphasising obedience, deference and sexual Puritanism. Theologically, it was a non-event: the church was about control, not speculation. Nowhere was its control more marked than in education. The union of nationalism and Catholic control of education had a long history, going back to the deal struck by the bishops with Parnell in the 1880s. By the 1920s, the arrangement was formalised by the new state and the church effectively took control of the Irish education system. The schools were owned and managed by the clergy but financed, for the most part, out of taxation.

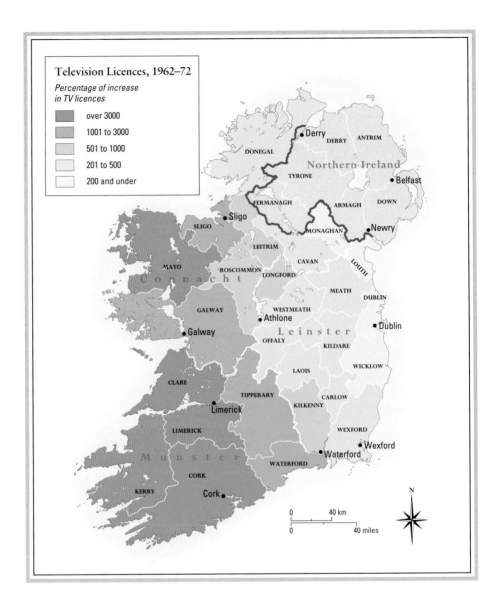

The education thus provided was overwhelmingly academic. Technical education was a discounted second best. The academic curriculum was a splendid vehicle for the preparation of priests, bureaucrats and self-reproducing pedagogues. Moreover, only primary education was free. Until 1968, secondary education had to be paid for, thus placing the working class at an enormous disadvantage. To be fair, some teaching orders – especially the Christian Brothers – had an honourable record of educating poorer boys. But the emphasis of the system was on social immobility. The possessor class held all the aces: its upper echelons went to relatively expensive 'private' schools and thereafter in smaller numbers to university, usually with the higher professions – medicine or law – in mind, or perhaps the management of such commercial activity as there was.

The lower echelons went to less advantaged schools but none the less could complete the secondary cycle in the expectation of a respectable place in the lower middle class, as bank clerks and such like.

Two groups were specifically and of necessity excluded from this process of minimal mobility. First, the urban working class was effectively outside it altogether. Most were condemned to semi-skilled or unskilled work at best, unemployment or emigration at worst. Even the skilled tradesmen, the aristocracy of labour, dropped out of formal education in their teens in order to serve their time to their trades. Indeed, they often served their time to their fathers' trades, for the craft unions operated a very effective closed shop at entry: another intelligent deployment of the possessor principle. In all, the working class represented a kind of ghetto, self-sufficient in many respects but marginal in terms of the positive power it exerted. For the most part, it could wield only negative power through trades unions.

Ian Paisley.

The second excluded group was the emigrants. Without emigration, the whole cosy stasis could not have succeeded for so long. Irish society never stopped deploring the evils of emigration while quietly profiting from its efficient function as a safety valve.

This petit bourgeois paradise was what ran up against the buffers in the late 1950s. In a sense, that was the last Victorian decade. Half a century after the death of the old queen, a vestige of the world she had left still subsisted – improbable as it might seem – in the poor republic to the west, once the closest part of her vast dominions. Economically and socially immobile, ostentatiously religious and mentally isolated, it was as if the first half of the twentieth century had happened somewhere else. Which, in fact, it had.

The changes that swept Ireland from the 1960s on need to be understood against this background. Turning the economy around was, in some ways, the easy bit. What was harder was the culture war. A new generation supplanted the aging revolutionaries and gradually there began a movement to re-insert Ireland in to the wider world, while allowing international influences in though ever more open doors. In some ways, it was a profoundly unheroic ambition: that Ireland should aspire to be just like anywhere else.

This explains why the new '60s middle class were much cooler nationalists than their predecessors and also why membership of what is now the European Union was probably the single project most tenaciously embraced by the '60s elite. It also explains why so much of the change in Ireland since the 1960s has focused on cultural rather than economic issues. The old economy was a busted flush and the whole country could quickly see the product of the reforms put in place after 1958. But the culture that sustained the old consensus was more enduring and focused above all on religious issues, particularly in the areas of sexual morality. The divorce and abortions referendums of the 1980s were a rancid low point in public discourse, with vicious rhetoric employed on both sides. Divorce was not approved by referendum until 1995 and then only by a margin of less than 1 per cent.

By the 1990s, however, the dam of clerical invincibility had already sprung a leak. Three years before the introduction of divorce, the bishop of Galway had been discovered to have fathered a child by an American divorcee. A few more priests – including one or two who were national media figures – were similarly discovered to be father in more senses than one. All this was faintly comic. What followed was not. Gradually, the full horror of the clerical sex abuse scandals began to emerge: the buggering and violating of minors by priests and brothers and the manner in which it was covered up by their superiors in the hierarchy. There is no doubt that these crimes were reported in some quarters with open glee: many in the media were post '60s liberals who disliked the church (to put it no stronger) and for them the hunt was now up. There was an unmistakeable air of 'we have the bastards now'. Yet have them they did, for there was no disguising or evading the truth.

The clerical abuse of minors had happened. It had not simply been a case of a few bad apples. It had been more widespread than anyone had imagined; it had been effectively tolerated and facilitated by a hierarchy more concerned for the integrity of the institutional church than for decency or justice. These crimes had been perpetrated by God's anointed, priests of a church that in sermons, pastorals and confessionals had always anathemised any form sexual incontinence, even when relatively innocent. There was nothing innocent about this. It all amounted to the most complete betrayal of trust. The observant, trusting faithful were left disorientated and bemused. Mass attendance, declining since the '60s, went into freefall. Vocations more or less ceased. The institution that had been the backbone of nationalist civil society since the 1820s, that had been at the apogee of its arrogant and self-assured power only a generation before, was subverted from within.

And as God exited left, Mammon entered right. The scandals of the 1990s coincided with the arrival of the Celtic Tiger. Ireland's baby boom had come late and a new generation born in the 1970s and early '80s suddenly found themselves growing up in a country roaring ahead with money and expectation. This was a phenomenon without precedent in modern Ireland. In a few years, it seemed that the wholesale embrace of Anglo-American capitalism – complete with its individualist and consumerist assumptions – had effectively replaced the church as the locus of authority and longing.

We need to retrace the key steps in this generational journey.

Charles Haughey.

De Valera was succeeded by Sean Lemass in 1959. He was the antithesis of de Valera. He had little charisma and projected the image of a competent technocrat. In fact, he had been the most energetic and intellectually daring of de Valera's ministers. He had put the tariff regime in place in the 1930s and had been its principal sponsor. But in the early '50s, when it still retained iconic status, he was the first leading figure in Fianna Fáil to question its wisdom.

As Taoiseach from 1959 to 1966, he presided over a startling reversal of policy and fortune. He adopted a plan drawn up by T. K. Whitaker, the secretary of the Department of Finance, which proposed the dismantling of tariff barriers and the introduction of inducements to draw in foreign capital in place of the obviously inadequate levels of domestic private investment. The plan developed into a government programme which mixed Keynesian economics, free trade and economic planning in a balance that was more pragmatic than intellectually coherent. However, it had two great merits. First, by pointing a way out of the mess the country was in, it lifted the sense of deep pessimism that had gripped the Republic in the 1950s. Second, it worked.

The economy grew by almost 20 per cent between 1958 and 1963. Exports grew 35 per cent by value. Although total employment did not increase in the

1960s, it changed its nature. Industrial employment increased to the point where it could absorb the rural surplus. Emigration practically stopped, for the first time since the Famine. The population, which had fallen at every census since the foundation of the state (except for one tiny and insignificant upward blip in 1951), increased successively in 1966 and 1971. By the latter date, it had recovered to the 1926 figure, thus reversing the haemorrhage of a generation.

The point about Irish economic growth in the 1960s is that it was no big deal by international standards. Ireland belatedly hitched a ride on the capitalist post-war boom. Success came from the intelligent application of conven-

Captain Terence O'Neill (left) and Sean Lemass (right) at one of their meetings in the mid-1960s.

tional international wisdom to local circumstances. This habit of borrowing from abroad became increasingly commonplace in the '60s: television, ecumenism, supermarkets: all made their entry in that decade. The one achievement that had the greatest effect on the future was the introduction of universal, free secondary schooling throughout the state in 1968.

There was a generational change, as the old revolutionaries retired and died. The new men were characterised by an energetic rejection of pessimism. Some in Fianna Fáil embraced a freebooting form of capitalism that had more than a whiff of third-world new money about it. Others were more deferential towards inherited pieties and correspondingly suspicious of rising stars like Charles Haughey, the most obviously able of the young Turks. A small but important liberal middle class formed which was influential in the media and the universities. Some of them, looking for a political home and failing to find it in the ripsnorting populism of the new Fianna Fáil, preferred the more genteel embrace of a Fine Gael that now found itself pulled between an international liberal wing and its old domestic reactionaries. A similar form of colonisation gripped the Labour party, traditionally a trade union vehicle, which now found that it had some radical chic bourgeoisie aboard.

There were great set pieces: John F. Kennedy visited in 1963, just months before his assassination, to embody the material achievements of the post-Famine diaspora. The golden anniversary of the 1916 rising was celebrated with due ceremony. But that anniversary also reintroduced the serpent in the Irish garden: sectarian murder in the north. It was also the fiftieth anniversary of the Battle of the Somme, at which the UVF (otherwise the 36th Ulster Division) had suffered appalling casualties. This conjunction of anniversaries across the communal divide resulted in the re-formation of the UVF and the murder of two Catholic men and an elderly Protestant woman (burned to death in her own home in error).

Yet, at the time, this seemed to contemporaries a tragic renewal of the past rather than a pointer to the future. When Brookeborough had stood down in 1963, he had been succeeded by Captain Terence O'Neill, a big-house old Etonian. His more talented rival Brian Faulkner had the misfortune to be middle class rather than landed. Such distinctions still mattered in the antique world of Ulster unionism. O'Neill set a new tone, not quite of liberalism, but at least of cautious accommodation.

The most dramatic démarche of O'Neill's premiership came in 1965, when he invited Lemass to visit Belfast. Lemass had been markedly more conciliatory than de Valera on the partition issue: in keeping with his character, he regarded it as a problem to be resolved rather than a fundamental moral issue. He accepted O'Neill's invitation. The two men met in Belfast in January 1965,

Army and Garda on the border c. 1990.

with O'Neill reciprocating the following month. Other ministers followed. A North-South tourism committee was established and other cautious forms of cross-border co-operation were explored.

O'Neill was never fully in control of his party or of his people. In the party, Faulkner resented the manner in which the leadership had been denied him; others on the right objected to any softening of rhetoric towards Catholics and North-South contacts generally. Outside the party, the unionist ultras found a voice in the Rev. Ian Paisley, a dissident Presbyterian ranter. O'Neill sounded pretty pallid compared to the ultra-charismatic Paisley.

In January 1967, the Northern Ireland Civil Rights Association was formed. Its purpose was to fight discrimination on the grounds of equal citizenship. Implicitly, it accepted the position of Northern Ireland within the United

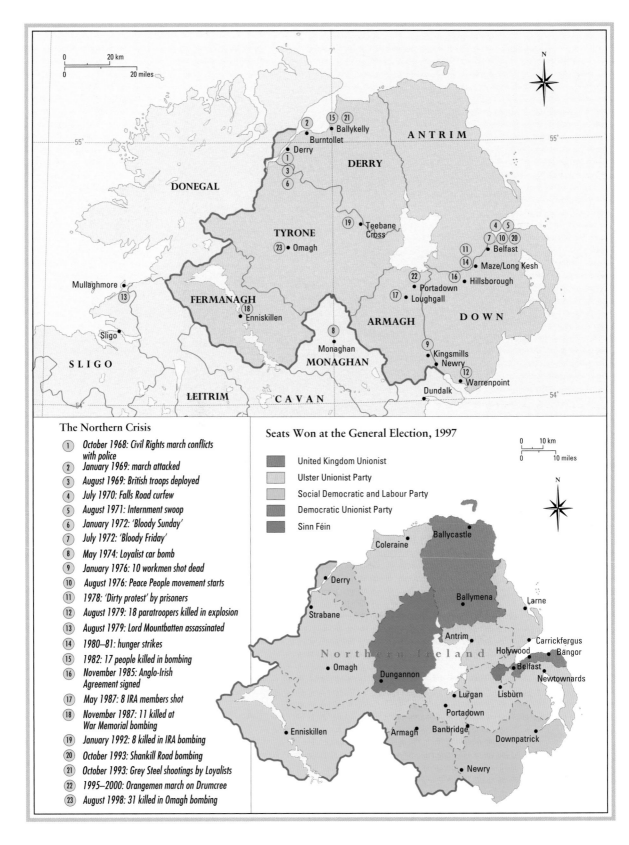

The Northern Crisis

1. October 1968: Civil Rights march conflicts with police
2. January 1969: march attacked
3. August 1969: British troops deployed
4. July 1970: Falls Road curfew
5. August 1971: Internment swoop
6. January 1972: 'Bloody Sunday'
7. July 1972: 'Bloody Friday'
8. May 1974: Loyalist car bomb
9. January 1976: 10 workmen shot dead
10. August 1976: Peace People movement starts
11. 1978: 'Dirty protest' by prisoners
12. August 1979: 18 paratroopers killed in explosion
13. August 1979: Lord Mountbatten assassinated
14. 1980–81: hunger strikes
15. 1982: 17 people killed in bombing
16. November 1985: Anglo-Irish Agreement signed
17. May 1987: 8 IRA members shot
18. November 1987: 11 killed at War Memorial bombing
19. January 1992: 8 killed in IRA bombing
20. October 1993: Shankill Road bombing
21. October 1993: Grey Steel shootings by Loyalists
22. 1995–2000: Orangemen march on Drumcree
23. August 1998: 31 killed in Omagh bombing

Seats Won at the General Election, 1997

United Kingdom Unionist
Ulster Unionist Party
Social Democratic and Labour Party
Democratic Unionist Party
Sinn Féin

Kingdom. The bogey of partition was thrust aside for the moment. The demand was for equal citizenship for all in the UK. This is not to deny that there were many republicans in the NICRA, happy to use it as a front: any lever would do to challenge unionist hegemony.

On 5 October 1968, the NICRA called a protest march in Derry. The Belfast administration, in the person of the Minister of Home Affairs, banned it. NICRA defied the ban. The RUC batoned the marchers off the streets. But unlike the old days, there were television cameras present. The pictures went round the world. This foetid little corner of the United Kingdom was about to become world news.

O'Neill called an election to get a new mandate but won only a Pyrrhic victory and resigned in April 1969. His successor was another plummy big-house gent, Major James Chichester-Clark, a nonentity. By the summer, Northern Ireland was ablaze. Months of civil disturbance

Gerry Adams.

followed the NICRA march, culminating in wholesale sectarian battles in Derry and Belfast in August. The residents of the Catholic Bogside ghetto in Derry fought the RUC to a standstill over three days. In Belfast, thousands of Catholics and some Protestants were burned out of their homes. Lemass's successor as Taoiseach, Jack Lynch, made a famously ambiguous television speech which might or might not have been a threat to intervene. In the end, it was the British Army that intervened, sent in a by a bemused and unwilling London government to keep the sides apart.

The explosion in Northern Ireland took almost everyone by surprise and caused an earthquake in Dublin. A high-level plan to import arms in support of beleagured northern nationalists was discovered. Lynch sacked two members of his cabinet whom he believed to be implicated, Charles Haughey and

Garret FitzGerald signing the Anglo-Irish Agreement with Prime Minister Margaret Thatcher in 1985.

the hard-line Donegal republican Neil Blaney. The courts tried them and others alleged to be involved: all were acquitted. The years 1969–72 were the rockiest in the history of Fianna Fáil, as it came face to face with the ambiguities of its history. The party's legendary instinct for unity held it together. The moderates around Lynch held the line. Blaney never rejoined the party; Haughey spent most of a decade in the wilderness rebuilding his support. Dublin was sympathetic to nationalist aspirations in Northern Ireland but it drew the line at overtly aiding and abetting the revived IRA.

The Republic joined the European Economic Community (now the EU) in 1972. It was the culmination of a decade of effort and preparation. The European project appealed principally to three groups: those who supported the new free trade economics that had enriched the South; the liberal intelligentsia; and, crucially, the farmers. This group was unconcerned about European idealism or Ireland emerging from behind the British shadow; they were, however, hugely attracted by the Common Agricultural Policy, which contrasted with Britain's cheap food policy and guaranteed prices to producers.

Europe appealed to cool nationalists like Garret FitzGerald, soon to be

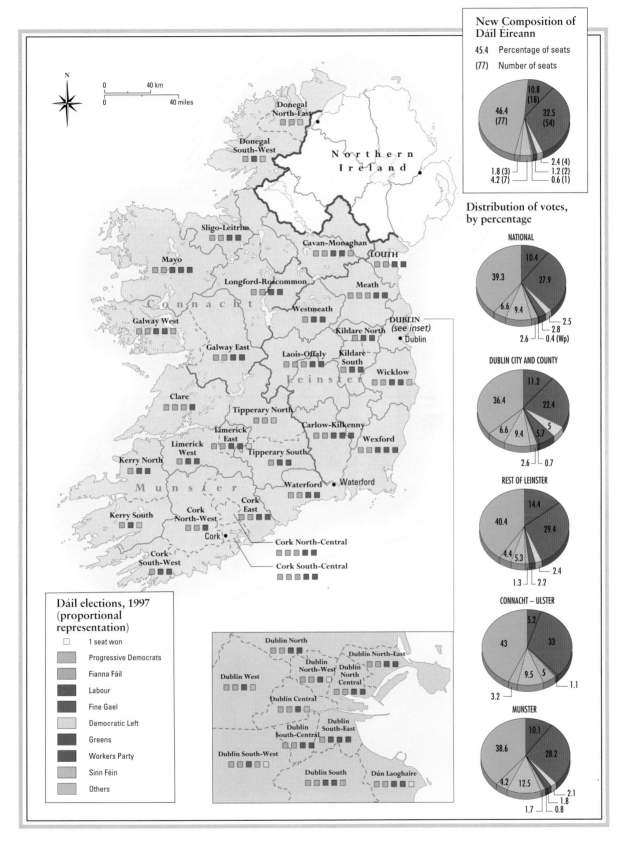

New Composition of
Dáil Éireann

45.4   Percentage of seats

(77)   Number of seats

10.8 (18)   32.5 (54)   46.4 (77)   2.4 (4)   1.2 (2)   0.6 (1)   1.8 (3)   4.2 (7)

Distribution of votes,
by percentage

NATIONAL

10.4   27.9   39.3   6.6   9.4   2.5   2.8   2.6   0.4 (Wp)

DUBLIN CITY AND COUNTY

11.2   22.4   36.4   6.6   9.4   5.7   5   2.6   0.7

REST OF LEINSTER

14.4   29.4   40.4   4.4   5.3   2.4   1.3   2.2

CONNACHT – ULSTER

5.2   33   43   9.5   5   1.1   3.2

MUNSTER

10.1   28.2   38.6   4.2   12.5   2.1   1.8   1.7   0.8

Dáil elections, 1997
(proportional
representation)

☐   1 seat won

Progressive Democrats

Fianna Fáil

Labour

Fine Gael

Democratic Left

Greens

Workers Party

Sinn Féin

Others

Donegal North-East

Donegal South-West

Sligo-Leitrim

Mayo

Cavan-Monaghan

LOUTH

Longford-Roscommon

Meath

Connacht

Westmeath

Galway West

Kildare North

DUBLIN (see inset)
• Dublin

Galway East

Laois-Offaly

Kildare South

Wicklow

Leinster

Clare

Tipperary North

Carlow-Kilkenny

Limerick East

Wexford

Limerick West

Tipperary South

Kerry North

Munster

Waterford
• Waterford

Kerry South

Cork East

Cork North-West

• Cork

Cork North-Central

Cork South-West

Cork South-Central

Northern Ireland

Dublin North

Dublin North-East

Dublin West

Dublin North-West

Dublin North Central

Dublin Central

Dublin South-East

Dublin South-Central

Dublin South-West

Dublin South

Dún Laoghaire

N

0   40 km

0   40 miles

Foreign Minister. Hot nationalists – the sort of people Lynch had sidelined in 1970 and others even more extreme – were generally opposed, hankering for the old simplicities of Sinn Féin autarky. The new generation of *soi disant* socialists in the Labour Party affected to oppose Europe on the grounds that it was a vast capitalist conspiracy. On examination, such people turned out over time to be bourgeois liberals all along: most revealed their genuine enthusiasm for the EU in due course. Real socialists and ultra nationalists – each out on the far margins of Irish life – continued to be the mainstay of anti-European feeling in Ireland until the development of the Green movement in the 1990s.

Membership of the EU has hugely enriched the Republic of Ireland. Farmers, most obviously, have profited from the grotesquely wasteful Common Agricultural Policy. EU social funds have been generously disbursed to bring the country's social infrastructure up towards continental standards and to aid hitherto neglected regions. Industrial exports found new markets. Inward investment, especially from the United States, expanded, as Ireland provided an anglophone access to European markets. The country's traditional dependence on Britain lessened to the point that Ireland entered the European Monetary System in 1979 although Britain stayed out. It meant breaking the link with

Omagh bomb, 1998.

sterling that had existed since 1826 (the currency union had survived independence) and reinstating an independent Irish currency. It lasted until the launch of the euro in 2002.

Entry into Europe was, in one sense, an admission of failure. The full aspiration of nationalism – for self-sufficiency and economic autonomy – had faltered. The nationalist adventure that began with O'Connell had either run out of steam or succeeded all too well, depending on how you read it. Going into Europe was abandoning the full nationalist impulse for a kind of benign imperialism. It certainly meant compromising sovereignty, although how much meaning that term has for a small, free-trading, open economy in a globalised world is open to question. It also re-connected Ireland to continental Europe in a manner not seen since the eighteenth century.

When the civil disturbances of 1969 reduced Northern Ireland to anarchy, the words 'IRA: I Ran Away' appeared on gable walls. The IRA had swung to the left in the 1960s, following the failure of the 1956–62 campaign and had come under the influence of a Dublin-based socialist leadership. There was a consequent emphasis on social action and lack of emphasis on traditional republican concerns. This proved costly when working-class Catholic ghettos came under attack from loyalist mobs, often aided and abetted by police and B Specials. The movement split. The left-wingers formed the Official IRA and the more traditional – and it must be said more practical – elements became the Provisional IRA. The Provos concentrated on community defence in the first instance – to purge the I Ran Away smear – and then moved on to a resumption of the 1920–22 civil war and an attempt to shoot and bomb the British out of Ireland altogether. The Fenian tradition had shrunk to the working-class ghettos of nationalist Northern Ireland, but was still alive and kicking.

Following 1969, the RUC began a rolling series of reforms that, no matter what they did, would never convince nationalists that they were anything other than a sectarian arm of the state. The B Specials were abolished. The local government franchise was reformed to end the sort of gerrymandering that obtained in Derry. It was too little too late. The Provos were set on their unwinnable war with the British, which they pursued for the best part of thirty years. They did enough, however, to ensure that they British could not defeat them.

The early troubles were enough to secure the resignation of Chichester-Clark and the elevation of Faulkner at last. Faulkner had been Minister of Home Affairs during the 1956–62 campaign and reckoned he knew how to deal with the IRA. In August 1971, he introduced internment. It was a botched job, based in part on faulty and out-of-date security information. But even if it had been a perfect operation, it would have remained a disastrous error of judgment. It massively increased nationalist alienation from the state and support for the Provos, whose operational capacity remained undiminished. The following year, 1972, was the most violent of the troubles, with 470 deaths, over 10,000 shooting incidents and almost 2,000 bomb explosions. In the same year, London closed the Belfast parliament and imposed direct rule.

The Provisional IRA represented the nationalist extreme. The mainstream was represented by the Social Democratic and Labour Party (SDLP) whose principal theoretician was John Hume from Derry. He preached a reconciliation of the two traditions through negotiation and movement towards an agreed future for both parts of Ireland. The SDLP was totally opposed to the violence of the IRA, not to mention the reciprocated assaults from loyalist paramilitaries.

In 1974, the British and Irish governments and the main Northern Ireland parties reached a deal at Sunningdale, near London, for a power-sharing, devolved government in Belfast. It also proposed a Council of Ireland, which was included at Dublin's insistence and over Faulkner's objections. The Executive was duly set up and lasted a mere five months. A British general election showed Faulkner's party to be badly split on power-sharing, with anti-Faulkner candidates doing best. Any legitimacy the Executive had in unionist eyes now evaporated. It was finally brought down by a general strike a few months later.

Thereafter, the troubles rumbled on from one atrocity and ambush to another, with dirty tricks on both sides. The deaths of ten republican hunger strikers in 1981 probably represented a psychological low point, although it also alerted the more intelligent people in the IRA and Sinn Féin that while the war could not be lost it could not be won either. Hunger strike candidates won by-elections and demonstrated the potential for political action. It took the best part of twenty years for this potential to transmute into practical politics. The republican movement was steeped in a culture of violence and would require much subtle persuasion to wean it off the gun. There were practical problems, of which the question of paramilitary prisoners was the most pressing (this consideration also affected loyalist groups). In the meantime, the troubles consumed 3,000 lives. The Provos' war – it was theirs, no one else's: they started it and when they stopped, the troubles stopped – grew out of the intolerable sectarian discrimination of the old unionist regime. But it soon acquired an ideological life of its own that went way beyond communal defence.

The most important political development of those years was the Anglo-Irish Agreement of 1985, signed by Margaret Thatcher for the UK and Garret FitzGerald for the Republic. It marked the beginning of a genuine rapprochement between Dublin and London and increased co-operation between the two governments. Crucially, it set up a joint ministerial conference supported by a permanent secretariat in Belfast. It stopped short of joint authority but gave Dublin a voice in the governance of Northern Ireland for the first time. Although it led to predictable unionist rage at a deal done over their heads, it created the conditions that made the peace process of the late 1990s possible. It also recognised the simple reality that more than one-third of the population of Northern Ireland had no loyalty to the state and had no reason to have any such loyalty.

The Republic mismanaged the economic legacy of the 1960s in the following decades. It was unlucky in that the world economy turned down following the oil crises of 1973 and 1979, but successive governments compounded their ill-luck by gross economic mismanagement. Charles Haughey staged a spectacular comeback to seize the leadership of Fianna Fáil and the office of Taoiseach in 1979, promising to clean things up. He only made them worse. Garret FitzGerald, by now leader of Fine Gael, produced his party's best-ever election performance in 1982 which allowed him to form a secure coalition with Labour. They began the job of rescuing the economy. This process accelerated on Haughey's return in 1987.

Gradually, the recovery policies worked, helped by the need to prepare the Irish economy for entry into the single European currency. Strict EU conditions had to be met. By the mid 1990s, Ireland had taken advantage of its geographical and linguistic position to become an offshore powerhouse of the American technology boom. It was this, more than anything, that underwrote the stunning economic success story of the Celtic Tiger in the years 1995 to 2001.

By then, a series of public enquiries had revealed a systematic maze of planning corruption and tax evasion among many prominent citizens from the '60s generation. Haughey himself was the most notable malefactor to be outed: he had lived for years like a prince on money donated by wealthy friends. And as we saw the Catholic church fell spectacularly from grace, hoist with its own petard: sex.

As early as 1988, John Hume, the leader of the SDLP and Gerry Adams, president of Sinn Féin, began a series of exploratory talks to see if a pan-nationalist consensus could be reached in Northern Ireland. The SDLP was the dominant group electorally: they out-polled Sinn Féin roughly two to one among nationalist voters. They were famously well-connected in Dublin, Washington and Brussels. It is worth recalling that, all through the troubles, a large majority of nationalists consistently denied electoral support to the political arm of the IRA. The talks were inconclusive at first but were resumed in 1993. They resulted in a document that Hume presented to the Dublin government of Albert Reynolds – Haughey's successor – who thought it sufficiently interesting to begin a démarche jointly with the British prime minister, John

European Union
*Development of the
European Community*

- Signature of the Treaty of Rome, 1957
- EEC member added 1973
- Greece added 1981
- EEC member added 1986
- Became part of the EEC after unification of Germany, 1990
- EEC member added 1995
- EEC member added 2004
- To be added 2007
- Membership pending

Major. This led to the Downing Street declaration of December 1993. A document of great subtlety, its essential importance lay in a British acknowledgment that the Irish people were entitled to a self-determination of their own future, thus diluting the claim to absolute sovereignty. The Irish government, for its part, conceded that any steps towards Irish unity could only be taken with the support of a majority in Northern Ireland, thus compromising the territorial claim in the 1937 constitution.

The declaration could not have happened without the Hume-Adams talks or, even more important, without the regular Dublin-London contacts now long established by the Anglo-Irish Agreement of 1985. It led to the IRA ceasefire of August 1994 which lasted until February 1996. The republican drift from violence to politics was painful: Adams demonstrated political skill of the highest order in facilitating the change without splitting the movement.

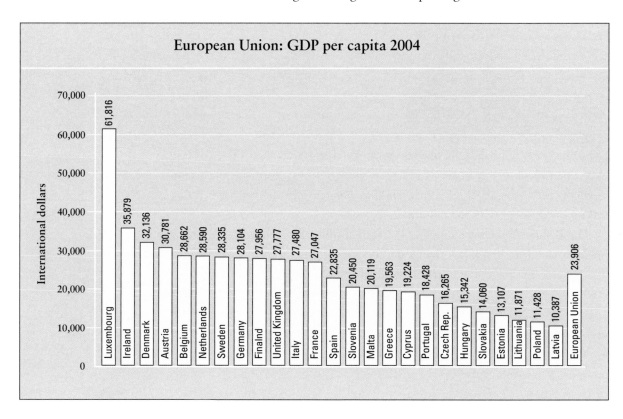

The drift towards peace eventually produced the Belfast Agreement of 1998, in which all parties – except the Paisleyite unionist ultras but including representatives of Sinn Féin and the two principal loyalist paramilitary groups – reached a nervous accommodation. The bones of the deal were as follows: the union with the UK would remain as long as a majority in Northern Ireland desired it; in return, there would be a devolved power-sharing executive and cross-border institutions to co-operate on matters of mutual concern; paramilitary violence of all sorts was to end; early release of paramilitary prisoners would be a priority.

Seamus Mallon, deputy leader of the SDLP, famously called it 'Sunningdale for slow learners'. Like Sunningdale, it was overwhelmingly endorsed by nationalists while dividing unionist opinion. It required the endorsement of both communities in Northern Ireland and of the electorate in the Republic. Nationalists on either side of the border did so readily. Ulster unionists showed no such certainty, many of them dismayed by what they regarded as rewarding IRA terrorism. Only a frantic campaign, involving British prime minister Tony Blair, American President Bill Clinton and even Nelson Mandela, produced a wafer-thin unionist consent.

In a formal sense, the troubles are over. But the inter-communal hatred that divides Protestant and Catholic in Northern Ireland persists. The province is as much a voluntary apartheid society as ever: different housing areas, different schools, different sports, different loyalties. Low-level sectarianism continues unabated, occasionally erupting virulently. Ceasefires or no, paramilitaries still control the ghettos and engage in beatings and knee-cappings of those who incur their displeasure. The distinction between political paramilitarism and gangsterism is not always clear: much of Northern Ireland's black economy and drugs trade flourishes on the ambiguity. As late as December 2004, the IRA were able to pull off the biggest bank robbery in post-war Europe while ostensibly engaged in negotiations – via their Sinn Féin surrogates – for a new political rapprochement with the unionists!

The Belfast Agreement remains the formal political anchor point, but in reality it is a dead letter, less than a decade after it was signed. It worked in a hesitant manner for a few years: a power-sharing executive was formed with David Trimble of the Ulster Unionist Party as first minister and Seamus Mallon of the SDLP as his deputy. It contained two Sinn Féin ministers. Paisley's DUP was not represented, since they rejected the entire process. It was bedevilled with tensions and distrust from the beginning, mainly focusing on the reluctance of the IRA to decommission its weapons, as it was obliged to do under the terms of the Belfast Agreement. Sinn Féin answered Unionist charges of bad faith on decommissioning by calling loudly for police reform.

The whole rickety arrangement collapsed finally in 2005. The British general election of that year saw the DUP sweep the boards on the unionist side, while Sinn Féin continued to outpace the SDLP on the nationalist side. Thus the extremes in both communities were now in command. More seriously, Paisley's triumph – and the virtual annihilation of the mainstream UUP – marked the effective withdrawal of Protestant consent to the Belfast

Agreement. That consent had been hesitant and feeble in any case. The perception among Protestants that all the concessions had been made to the other side with little received in return was enough to elevate Paisley to the leadership of unionism for the first time ever. Whether the two extremes can ever reach the sort of *modus vivendi* that eluded the mainstream parties is a moot question. At least the decommissioning issue was more or less laid to rest in 2005, when the IRA finally – if belatedly – destroyed enough of their arsenal to satisfy international observers.

As the two sides within Northern Ireland continue their historic stand-off, the two parts of the island are moving farther apart than ever. The southern economy finally roared into life in the 1990s, with the Republic achieving spectacular rates of economic growth. From 1991 to 2003, the average annual growth rate was almost 7 per cent, peaking at a vertiginous 11 per cent in 1999. After a brief hiccup in 2002 and 2003, the exceptional boom returned from 2004.

What caused this transformation in a country previously known for economic under-achievement? In one sense, this way of posing the question suggests part of the answer. The Republic was coming from farther back than it should have been: there was simply more ground to be made up and therefore more scope for growth. The eventual rectification of the national finances after the profligate '70s and '80s was an essential pre-condition. The lowest level of corporation tax in the EU gave the country a key competitive advantage for the attraction of inward investment, which was most visible in the IT sector. A well-educated young Anglophone population also helped. So did a policy of social partnership, in which government, employers and trades unions negotiated centralised multi-annual agreements, thus making Ireland one of the most stable labour environments in the world. The cost of employing labour was significantly lower than in most other EU countries and a policy of low personal taxation moved the country decisively towards the American model of capitalism.

As with America, the price paid for all this was increasing inequality: those left behind in the boom are farther back than ever, and this has contributed to an underlying sense of unease. And certain areas are still chronically problematic, notably the health and transport systems.

None the less, it is hard to argue for long with a process that has reduced unemployment from 18 per cent when Charles Haughey was Taoiseach in the 1980s to 4 per cent in Bertie Ahern's Ireland of the new century. The consequences have been spectacular. The country is visibly richer. Car ownership – a key indicator of consumer buoyancy – has doubled since 1980 and now approaches the EU average. There has been a spectacular boom in house prices, which have grown to ten times their early '90s values at a time when inflation has been low. This has made millions of Irish people asset rich in a manner beyond their dreams. Interest rates are low, facilitating easy credit – too easy, some would say.

It is not just the Irish themselves that are impressed with all this. A country that half a century ago was haemorrhaging emigrants is now a magnet for immigrants. These are not just the Irish abroad coming home to a better country, as was the case with the net immigration of the late '60s and early '70s. People have flocked into Ireland to work in the course of the boom. Immigrants vote with their feet: their presence is the greatest vote of confidence a country can have. There are over 100,000 Poles in Ireland, for example, and their numbers are being augmented by a regular bus service from Warsaw to Dublin. The capital's evening newspaper, the *Evening Herald*, has a weekly section in Polish. It is a commonplace, no longer worth remarking on, to be served by an immigrant in a pub, restaurant or hotel. No one turns a hair at the sound of a foreign language. The building boom that is gripping twenty-first century Ireland would not be possible without skilled and semi-skilled immigrant labour.

One company more than any other symbolises the sheer swagger of Celtic Tiger Ireland. In 1990, Ryanair was five years old and had accumulated losses of £20 million. In 2006, it is long established as the biggest low-fares airline in Europe, where it has completely revolutionised air travel. In 1991, it crept into profit and carried 650,00 passengers. In 2005, it carried 35 million passengers on 288 routes and posted a profit of almost 270 million Euros. It is one of the most recognised online brands in the world. It has done this in the teeth of official discouragement – neither government nor national flag carrying airlines were exactly supportive – and by copying a business model first developed in the United States. Once again, the Celtic Tiger draws its influence from across the Atlantic at a time when tensions between Europe and the United States have seldom been stronger. Indeed, weakening support for the EU in Ireland – a 1998 referendum on an EU treaty was actually lost in Ireland, something hitherto unthinkable – almost certainly reflects the headlong embrace of American cultural and economic values.

In 1780 or so, Ireland was part colony, part periphery in the world of the ancien régime. By the early twenty-first century, democracy and popular sovereignty had so replaced aristocratic privilege that they were taken totally for granted. The island survived a terrible demographic catastrophe, the Famine, in the mid-nineteenth century. It was partitioned in the early twentieth, as nationalism and unionism were irreconcilable. In the Ulster redoubt, it is still so. The rest of the island is a republic, a member of the European Union but culturally tied ever more to the Anglo-American world. In 1780, Ireland was united and poor. Now, it is divided and rich.

Whatever the future holds, the story of modernisation in Ireland contains fragments of experience that are unique to the island and its circumstances and others that are typical of a process that has swept the entire world in that time. No historical record is completely unique. The Irish may be distinctive, but are also just people. Under similar stresses, people everywhere tend to respond in similar fashions. This is particularly so on islands, open as they are to external influence. A national history inevitably will emphasise features that are thought different – even unique – about a country's experience. But that insular need to borrow is also there and is a recurring theme in the story that is now stopping

not ending. Ireland borrowed at different times from French republicanism, from English social and educational models, from Westminster politics, from German romantic nationalism, from American popular culture. The most important borrowing of all has been language. Modern Ireland's thoughts and dreams have been willingly formulated in the language of the conqueror. Most of its literature, the cultural achievement for which Ireland is best known, has been in English. There have been inevitable regrets, often passionately articulated, at the loss of Irish. The argument that Ireland has been culturally disabled by its language shift has found few takers in the street. Instead, the gains that have accrued from speaking English have been banked with gratitude. No change has been more fundamental than that.

Ryanair Boeing 737 taking off.

*Cranes in Dublin's
dockland skyline.*

A L'ARMÉE FRANÇAISE,

DESTINÉE

A OPÉRER LA RÉVOLUTION D'IRLANDE.

RÉPUBLICAINS,

FIER de vous avoir fait vaincre en plusieurs occasions, j'ai obtenu du Gouvernement la permission de vous conduire à de nouveaux succès. Vous commander, c'est être assuré du triomphe.

Jaloux de rendre à la liberté un peuple digne d'elle, et mûr pour une révolution, le Directoire nous envoie en Irlande, à l'effet d'y faciliter la révolution que d'excellents Républicains viennent d'y entreprendre. Il sera beau pour nous, qui avons vaincu les satellites des Rois armés contre la République, de briser les fers d'une Nation amie, de lui aider à recouvrer ses droits usurpés par l'odieux gouvernement anglais.

Vous n'oublierez jamais, braves et fidèles Compagnons, que le Peuple, chez lequel nous allons, est l'ami de notre Patrie, que nous devons le traiter comme tel, et non comme un peuple conquis.

En arrivant en Irlande, vous trouverez l'hospitalité, la fraternité ; bientôt des milliers de ses habitans viendront grossir nos phalanges. Gardons-nous donc bien de jamais traiter aucuns d'eux en ennemis. Ainsi que nous, ils ont à se venger des perfides Anglais ; ces derniers sont les seuls dont nous ayons à tirer une vengeance éclatante. Croyez que les Irlandais ne soupirent pas moins que vous après le moment où, de concert, nous irons à Londres rappeler à Pitt et à ses amis, ce qu'ils ont fait contre notre liberté.

Par amitié, par devoir, et pour l'honneur du nom français, vous respecterez les personnes et les propriétés du pays où nous allons. Si, par des efforts constans, je pourvois à vos besoins, croyez que, jaloux de conserver la réputation de l'Armée que j'ai l'honneur de commander, je punirai sévèrement quiconque s'écartera de ce qu'il doit à son pays. Les lauriers et la gloire seront le partage du soldat républicain ; la mort sera le prix du viol et du pillage. Vous me connoissez assez pour croire que, pour la première fois, je ne manquerai pas à ma parole. J'ai dû vous prévenir, sachez vous en rappeller.

Le Général,

L. HOCHE.

Brest, le   année républicaine.

—————— CHAPTER 12 ——————

CONTINUITIES AND DISJUNCTIONS
The Collision of History and Myth

History is a search for such truths as we can recover from the past. Alternatively, it is the recasting of the past to suit the conveniences of the present. It is never neutral or complete.

The study of history as a formal academic discipline is little more than a hundred years old.

Very few historians are consciously biased or partisan in their selection of material or their use of sources. Nearly all aspire to fairness, balance and some degree of neutrality in the face of contentious issues. All understand very well that a perfect objectivity is impossible. We are prisoners of our presents as well as of our pasts. Inevitably, current political predispositions will colour our interpretations of the past. How lurid the colouring is depends on the individual.

If the pseudo-scientific study of history is a relatively recent thing, myth is as old as mankind. Myths, fables and paradigms go back to Homer and beyond. They have an enduring quality. The greatest novelist of the twentieth century, searching for a template within which his description of a day in the life of a modern man might be contained, found it in Homer's *Odyssey*. The result was James Joyce's *Ulysses*.

Myth is anterior to history. It satisfies a greater, more primordial human need. It furnishes us with folk tales, fictions, fantasies. It speaks to the human imagination. Without myth, there can be no literature.

Historians are often at war with myths. For all the shortcomings of historians noted above, their craft is one that aspires to discover truths. Frequently, these are truths that are occluded behind a myth or displaced altogether by it. A recent example of this phenomenon has been the re-examination of the myth of heroic French resistance to the Third Reich. Revisionist historians have discovered that, far from the officially sanctioned narrative of the French Resistance, the quotidian reality was rather grubbier. There were many collaborators, some of them enthusiastic anti-Semites. There were millions who meekly submitted to the Germans, knowing all too well the ferocious punishments for any infractions. The Resistance itself was disproportionately the work of the young – those without

Far Left: French Revolutionary Proclamation.

199

Far Right: A proclamation issued by the French force, under General Jean Humbert, which landed at Kilcummin Bay, near Killala in County Mayo, on 22 August 1798.

full adult responsibilities – and Communists, possessed of a quasi-religious system of belief. After the war, de Gaulle needed to take ownership of the Resistance from the Communists: thus he was the principal mover in creating a deeply comforting myth for his countrymen, which represented them not as timid collabos but as heroic enemies of tyranny.

It was a good and useful myth. As T.S. Eliot noted, people can take only so much reality. In 1945, France was recovering from the most shattering defeat in her history. The country needed the comfort of an enabling narrative, one which became an article of faith right through the *trente glorieuses*, the thirty years of economic and social recovery that followed. It was only when that recovery was complete, by the 1970s, that historians and journalists began to poke around the edges of the myth and eventually to subvert it. This revisionism was resented, partly because people want to believe the best of themselves, partly because people understood that the myth had a practical as well as a symbolic value.

Yet subverted it was. Rather like the scorpion that bit the frog which had just carried it safely across a river, the historian might have said: "it's my nature". Sooner or later, the urge to learn the truth behind comforting tribal myths proves irresistible. This makes the historian an awkward customer, because he can disturb beliefs cherished and long-held by an entire community. To be fair, he will generally not do this until the time is right, until there is a constituency within the community which is receptive to his heresies. He therefore catches the tide of a social or generational change and begins the formulation of a new, replacement orthodoxy that will be subverted in its turn.

In doing this, the historian faces not just the hostility of those who hold onto myths for their comfort value. He also suffers from his distance from the events described, the incompleteness of written sources, the unreliability of surviving witnesses and so on. He aspires to the truth, or at least a version of it, in the knowledge that the aspiration is never fully realisable. He also knows, if he is wise, that the myth is not the same thing as a lie and that his enterprise is at bottom a contest between the reason and the imagination. In this contest, the imagination holds the best cards. Myth is anterior to history. Which brings us back to Ireland.

How do nations begin? The myth usually proposes a timeless tribal continuity. In the Irish case, this means the direct association of the modern nation with a continuous cultural and political integrity going all the way back to the pre-Christian Celts. All those who subsequently disturbed the Celtic order – Vikings in the ninth century, Normans in the twelfth, New English and Cromwellians in the sixteenth and seventeenth – were seen as interlopers, strangers in the house. This perception could coincide with the view of the Gaels as absorbers of strangers who would become "more Irish than the Irish themselves". But the point was that it was the Gaels that did the absorbing, not they who dissolved into

ERTY, EQUALITY, FRATERNITY, UNIO

IRISHMEN,

YOU have not forgot Bantry bay. You know what efforts France has made to assist you.

Her affection for you, her desire of avenging your wrongs and assuring your independence can never be impaired.

After several unsuccessfull attempts, behold at last Frenchmen arrived amongst you.

They come to support your courage, to share your dangers, to join their arms and to mix their blood with yours in the sacred cause of liberty.

They are the forerunners of other Frenchmen, whom you shall soon enfold in your arms.

Brave IRISHMEN, our cause is common. Like you we abhor the avaricious and blood-thirsty policy of an oppressive governement. Like you we hold as indefeasible the right of all nations to liberty. Like you we are persuaded that the peace of the world shall ever be troubled as long as the British ministry is suffered to make with impunity a traffic of the industry, labour and blood of the people.

But exclusive of the same interests which unite us, we have powerfull motives to love and defend you.

Have we not been the pretext of the cruelty exercised against you by the Cabinet of S. James? The heart-felt interest you have shown for the grand events of our revolution, has it not been imputed to you as a crime? Are not tortures and death continually hanging over such of you as are barely suspected of being our friends?

Let us unite then and march to glory.

We Swear the most inviolable respect for your properties, your laws and all your religions opinions. Be free, be masters in your own country. We look for no other conquest than that of your Liberty, no other success than your

The ... making your chains is arrived. Our triumphant troops are now flying ... nities of the earth to tear up the roots of the wealth and tyranny of ... es. That frightfull colossus is mouldering away in every part. Can ... ny Irishman ba ... ough to seperate himself in such a happy conjunct ... the grand int ... of his country. If su ... re be, brave friends, let him be chased from the ... try he betrays and let his property become the reward of those generous men who know how to fight and die.

Irishmen, recollect the late defeats wich your ennemies have experienced from the French; recollect the plains of Honscoote, Toulon, Quiberon and Ostende; recollect America free from the moment she wished to be so. The contest between you and your oppressors can not be long.

Union, Liberty, the Irish Republic. Such is our shout. Let us march. Our hearts are devoted to you; our glory is in your happiness.

another's culture. Indeed, D.P. Moran, the editor of *The Leader* in the early years of the twentieth century, did not put a tooth in it: "the foundation of Ireland is the Gael, and the Gael must be the element that absorbs".

But most nations did not start like that. France began as the royal demesne lands in the Ile de France and gradually, over centuries, pushed ever outward to absorb peripheral territories whether by marriage or conquest. The modern hexagonal shape of the country was not complete until 1648. Likewise Britain, a multi-national kingdom in which the English element first subsumed Wales in the 1530s and Scotland in 1707. Even within England, however, the king's writ did not run uncontested throughout his nominal territories until Tudor times. Spain created peninsular unity by internal conquest, but the primacy of the centre has always been contested, especially in Catalonia and the Basque country. Portugal secured and maintained its outright independence of Castile. Italy and Germany managed to create no unitary state at all until the second half of the nineteenth century despite shared cultural and linguistic legacies. States that appear secure and certain in their historical formation are often not so at all and are highly contingent constructions.

This book has placed a significant emphasis on the importance of the Catholic community in the south east of Ireland in the making of the modern Irish nation. Not quite as a glamorous as the king of France pushing ever outward from the Ile de France, it none the less seems to me to have been an analogous process. The special circumstances created by the political and industrial revolutions of the late eighteenth century created a new idea of the state. Sixteenth- and seventeenth-century heroes like Hugh O'Neill, Hugh O'Donnell or Patrick Sarsfield were not 'dying for Ireland' in the sense that Patrick Pearse would have understood the term, because the Ireland that Pearse understood was not yet born or thought of. The great continuity with O'Neill, O'Donnell and Sarsfield is not Ireland but Roman Catholicism.

Irish nationalism is the product of the Catholic community, originally divided ethnically between Gaels and Anglo-Normans (better known as the Old English). The ethnic division was occluded by Cromwell's failure to acknowledge it, and thereafter the Irish problem became the island's inability to fold into the pan-Protestant British state, as Protestant Wales and Protestant Scotland had done. (Their acceptance of Britishness was not always comfortable, but it stuck, only becoming a problem when Britishness became confused with Englishness. It would have been a brave man in any age who would have called a Welshman or a Scot 'English'.)

The fact that most of Ireland did not embrace the Reformation was decisive. Religion has always been the elephant in the Irish room. The gradual outward push of the English crown to absorb all of England, Scotland and Wales came to a halt in Ireland. From the Reformation onward, some form of challenge to the legitimacy of English rule was seldom far away. The illegitimacy of the Cromwellian land settlement of the 1650s in the eyes of the dispossessed was central to these challenges. The overwhelming fact was that land had been taken from Irish Catholics and handed over to English Protestants. There was no evading this simple reality, as John Fitzgibbon – the pro-Union lord chancellor of the late eighteenth century – understood so well. It was equally well understood by subsequent generations of Catholics, for whom it furnished the central grievance of their enterprise. It is no surprise that Irish nationalism for most of the nineteenth century was focused on the land question, that the settlement of the issue – in effect, the reversing of the Cromwellian plantations – aroused more nationalist passion than any other and that, when the goal was finally achieved in 1903, much of the steam went out of traditional parliamentary nationalism.

That nationalism had arisen in the particular context of the French revolution, from which democratic doctrines of popular sovereignty derived. The community that defined itself in national terms was the Catholic one, thus effecting a historic union of confessional grievance with the new-fangled theory of the national state. That was not something that just happened: it required social leadership, as all revolutions do. It found it among the rich Catholics of the south east – most of them descendants of dispossessed Old English who had done well in trade and commerce. It was they who furnished the educated, self-assured leadership of the emergent nation in disproportionate numbers.

But like post-war France, the emerging Irish nation needed an enabling myth and it got it in the image of faith and fatherland. Sedulously propagated by O'Connell and all later nationalists, it associated the Irish nation not only with the entire Catholic community but with an unbroken tradition of resistance to 'the stranger in the house' going back to time immemorial. Despite occasional bouts of nationalist bad conscience over the Catholic bit – there was the odd nod towards the memory of poor Wolfe Tone and his non-sectarian idealism – it seldom took long for essentials to re-assert themselves. To this day, the association between nationalism and Catholicism in Northern Ireland is almost complete.

Ah yes, Northern Ireland. Here is the contested ground where two myths meet. In the words of one historian, Northern Ireland is a classic 'ethnic frontier', similar to those places in the Balkans with which the world became so familiar after the fall of Communism. Two (or more) peoples of different tribal provenance but sharing a common language are none the less divided by more fundamental allegiances. It seems that the most fundamental of these is religion. The clearest lines of division in the Balkans are between Latin Christians (Slovenes and Croats), Orthodox Christians (Serbs and Montenegrins) and Muslims (parts of Bosnia and Kosovo). In Northern Ireland, the division is between the two principal varieties of Latin Christianity, Roman Catholicism (nationalists) and Protestantism (unionists).

These primary divisions run in a rough parallel to others. The Protestants are broadly divided between Calvinists and Anglicans, reflecting the ethnic origins of the original seventeenth-century planters. The Scots were Calvinist/Presbyterian, the English Anglican. The long eighteenth-century ascendancy of the established Church – the Anglican Church of Ireland – resulted in a sense of resentment and exclusion among Presbyterians that has echoes to this day. Of course, given the extremely fissiparous nature of Northern Ireland Protestantism – there are reckoned to be more than 40 competing churches, meeting houses and gospels halls of one sort or another on Belfast's Shankill Road alone – this basic Anglican-Presbyterian dichotomy is not the whole story. That said, it is the original basis for a community with a culture of internal disputation and division, capable of uniting only in times of extreme external threat. Such a time was the early years of the twentieth century, when the Protestants of Ulster faced the prospect of being incorporated into a devolved, regional all-Ireland parliament in which the Catholic majority on the whole island would inevitably dominate. Their opposition to this plan was so ferocious that it resulted in the partition of Ireland, with Northern Ireland being carved out of six of the nine counties of Ulster, the six which guaranteed a local Protestant majority.

The creation of the Protestant statelet reflected a mythical self-regard in the community, in which Ulster Protestants saw themselves as a providential people, a tribe of the elect set down in a barbarous land which it was their destiny to claim for civilisation. This sort of overheated communal solipsism had a long pedigree on the farther shores of European Protestantism. The Anabaptists in sixteenth-century Germany – in the first generation of the Reformation – thought of themselves as an elect set apart from ordinary humanity. In the next century, many of the extreme English revolutionary sectarians – the Levellers, Diggers, Fifth Monarchy Men and all the rest – were of a similar disposition. Most dramatically, so were the New England Puritans who founded America. As late as the 1980s, President Ronald Reagan could refer to his country as "a shining city on a hill", echoing the famous quotation from John Winthrop, one of the most influential of the early colonists, in a speech in1630: "For we must consider that we shall be as a City upon a hill. The eyes of all people are upon us. So that if we shall deal falsely with our God in this work we have undertaken, and so cause him to withdraw his present help from us, we shall be made a story and a byword throughout the world."

This sort of sentiment found a ready echo in post-Plantation Ulster. The new settlers were pioneers in a hostile land. Following the Flight of the Earls in 1607 – in which the traditional Gaelic lords of the province had decamped to the continent – large numbers of their former tenants were left behind, now to be tenants to their new masters or to be pushed to marginal, less productive uplands. The colonists were alien in language, ethnicity and religion – and the greatest of these was religion. The long historical interchanges between Ulster and Scotland, which might have been thought to modify differences, were deceptive. The planters were Lowland Scots, themselves bitterly hostile to the Gaelic tribes of the Highlands and Islands who formed a united seaborne culture with Gaelic Ulster. The basis of Lowland hostility to the Highlands was ethnic: the Lowlands were largely Norman, the Highlands Gaelic. This basic division was overlain by the Lowland embrace of Calvinism – thereafter the very core of Scottish difference – while the Highlands, like Gaelic Ulster, held fast to the old faith.

For the Lowlanders who planted Ulster in the early seventeenth century, therefore, their new country was still populated by the cousins of their historical enemies, whom they despised as an ignorant and backward people. The subsequent development of modern agricultural methods and the rise of towns in Ulster – Protestant achievements both – did little to shake the superiority of the Ulster Protestants. The process was completed by the stunning manner in which the Industrial Revolution took hold in nineteenth-century Ulster, while the Catholic South starved in the Famine. Memories and myths of the Catholic rebellion of 1641 were constantly recalled, esepcially the ugly massacre of settlers. The numbers were sedulously exaggerated for propaganda purposes, as if the facts themselves were not bad enough. The propaganda did its job, furnishing Protestant Ulster with its myth of Catholic treachery. God's people, set to do His work in a fallow land, must always and forever be alert to the traitors and murderers within.

And so, in 1920, they got their own little state. In effect, the only part of Ireland that did not want home rule got it. And they made the most of their opportunity according to their lights. Sadly, their lights were very dim indeed. Northern Ireland became a forcing house for every kind of small-minded suburban bigotry, in which tribal and national differences were magnified at every hand's turn. In essence, the statelet treated its 35 per cent Catholic minority as a fifth column and indulged the two generations of self-important Mr Toads who were its Protestant rulers. No effort was made to reconcile the Catholics of Northern Ireland to the partition state: the civil war in Ulster between the two sides in 1920–22, itself the renewal of centuries of hostility and mistrust, would have made the task difficult (to put it mildly). But not one significant Ulster Unionist politician even tried until it was all too late. Politics atrophied. Elections were just flag waving exercises on both sides and the results no more than sectarian headcounts. Where there were local Catholic majorities in the western part of the statelet, the Unionists gerrymandered the constituencies. The place was permanently governed by emergency legislation.

To the Catholics of the Republic, as the 26 counties of the Free State eventually became, partition was an affront. For their co-religionists in Northern Ireland, it was a disaster in which they were delivered into the hands of their enemies. These degrees of difference begin to explain the response of the South to partition.

Irish nationalism was grounded in an assertion of insular unity. Ireland was and always had been a nation from the centre to the sea, from north to south and east to west: the merest glance at a map would demonstrate the unity that nature had made. It was an axiom that the island of Ireland was a geographical and historical unity.

Partition, however, was a pretty blunt denial of this axiom. Presented with this irreversible denial the South was thrown back on rhetoric. When faced with the reality of the unionist presence, and its concentration in numbers in the north-east of this island, and the inability of nationalism to do anything about it, nationalism resorted to name calling.

Irish nationalism has never known what to do about the unionists, or what to make of them. There is, of course, the official fantasy position: that if Britain abandoned them to their fate they would suddenly realise that the jig is up and would stop living in bad faith. Instead, they would discover that they were true Irish people all along. Pigs will fly in orderly squadrons before that fairy tale comes true.

Irish nationalism, in its living, breathing form, begins with O'Connell. As early as 1828, O'Connell approved the initiative of Honest Jack Lawless to try to extend the reach of the Catholic Association to Ulster, where it was organisationally more or less non-existent (see page 44). This was 'the invasion of Ulster'. At Ballybay, Co. Monaghan, on the southern reaches of Ulster, the 'invasion' was turned back by an Orange mob. This moment, where Catholic numbers meet serious Protestant resistance for the first time in southern Ulster, set a pattern for the next two centuries.

It is the adamantine quality of Ulster Protestant resistance that is so infuriating for nationalists. It defies the sentimental axiom of insular unity. That, and the fact that the unionists' political culture is grounded in a thoroughly unpleasant supremacism which would not have been out of place in Bloemfontein or Alabama in the 1950s. They are hard to like, not just for nationalists, but for most modern people.

So it is easy to call them names. It is easy to say that theirs is an infantile political culture; that their capacity for sheer, unredeemed religious bigotry is breathtaking; that their political vocabulary contains only one word – no – and requires advanced speech therapy; that the swaggering of the Orange bullies is an affront to modernity and decency alike. And so on: make your own list. It will sound good and it will play well in most places. Much of it is perfectly true. It is, however, the rhetoric of impotence.

It has a pedigree. P.T. Ginley of Sinn Fein said in 1925 that "nobody had a right to mutilate Ireland, and least of all that little body of foreign colonists in the north-east … whose forbears had come to this country for robbery and spoliation." Well, right or not right, they did it anyway and the Ginleys of the world were powerless before them. James Connolly had famously told a Belfast Orange heckler who brandished a copy of the Ulster Solemn League and Covenant at him to take it home and frame it, that his children would laugh at it. As Conor Cruise O'Brien acidly remarks: "the children have not laughed, nor are the grandchildren laughing".

When you hear this kind of thing, you know that nationalism has bumped up against the same basic reality that baulked Honest Jack Lawless in Ballybay. There is strength in numbers, and surely the real infantilism in unionism is that they themselves so seldom see it. The state of constant hysteria in which unionism subsists, seeing sellouts and betrayals in the merest concessions, is debilitating.

Mainstream nationalism has long accepted partition, however reluctantly, as the practical limit of what can be achieved. The Northern policy of every Dublin administration since the outbreak of the Troubles has been accomodation, whether out of conviction (Lynch and FitzGerald et al) or *faute de mieux* (Haughey). It is accepted, but never admitted, that nationalism is co-terminus with the areas of overwhelming Catholic population. Where Catholic numbers falter, so does nationalism. Where they recover, as increasingly they do in Northern Ireland west of the Bann, unionism finds itself in retreat.

But there are enough Protestants in concentrated numbers, even in their shrinking space, to frustrate nationalist ambitions indefinitely. The demographic optimists who suppose that a Catholic majority of 50 per cent plus one in Northern Ireland will finish the job are deluding themselves. When and if that day comes – and demographers are bitterly divided on the matter – the problem of how to accommodate unionism will not have gone away.

There is one footnote to all this. Ulster has always been different. Even on small islands, there can be no blithe assumption of social or geographical unity. It is not necessary to quote the obvious examples of Hispaniola or New Guinea: Cyprus – only a fraction the size of Ireland – furnishes an eloquent European example. Indeed, the notional unity of the island of Great Britain is itself contingent and increasingly contested in Scotland and Wales. The Irish nationalist assertion of unity – the emotional tap root of the myth – is flawed. Even in the late Gaelic era, in the fifteenth and sixteenth centuries, Ulster was the most remote and inaccessible part of the island. Its natural southern boundary, a teasing daisy-chain of lakes and low hills called drumlins that stretches from the Irish Sea to the Atlantic, affords few points of entry to the invader. Ulster lived behind this natural fortress for most of its history, cut off from the rest of the island by near impossible land transportation, while its seaborne connection with the Scottish highlands and islands sustained a maritime mini-empire of which St Columba, the Ulsterman who was the Christian apostle of Scotland and Northern England, was the most prominent exemplar.

The remoteness and inaccessibility of Ulster was no joke. Look at the magnificent map of Ireland made by the cartographer Baptista Boazio in 1599 or that by Van der Keere from the same decade, reproduced opposite. Both render the island south of the Dublin-Galway line with remarkable fidelity, considering that they had no access to modern surveying methods. The southern half of Ireland was a geographical known: even distant places like the western Munster peninsulas are rendered in a recognizable manner. The northern half of the island, in contrast, is a mess. Boazio and his contemporaries simply did not have the information: this was terra incognita. Lough Erne, on the south-western reaches of Ulster, is shown as being twice the size of Lough Neagh, deep in the Ulster heartland, when the reality is the exact opposite. But Lough Erne was known – or at least close to the known world – while Lough Neagh was away below the Ulster horizon. The cartographers knew that there was a large body of water there somewhere. They got the location about right and the size – Lough Neagh is the largest body of inland water in the British Isles – completely wrong. Little wonder that Elizabeth I's crown troops kept getting beaten up by Hugh O'Neill in the south Ulster marchlands in the 1590s. The poor devils were lost, while O'Neill knew exactly where he was.

The particularism of Ulster subsisted even in the Gaelic world after the Plantation. The dialect of Irish spoken there is significantly different to this day. As we saw (page 130) hurling in Ulster was different to the game further south and was made to conform to it by the process of internal imperialism that was the early GAA. The Catholic population is ethnically Gaelic to a hugely disproportionate degree, with little of the Old English cross-pollination that was so important in the south. To all this regional difference, the Plantation of Ulster merely added. But it added it in a degree that made any insular unity impossible. In effect, the real border is along the line of the River Bann. East of here, the Anglo-Scots world begins; west of it, the Gaelic/Irish world.

Scotland ends, not at the Mull of Kintyre, but at the Bann. Nationalist Ireland faces it on the western bank. This is a hateful thought for nationalist and unionist alike. Both have indulged myths and fantasies for generations, which have sustained the imaginative integrity of both communities. But the myths and fantasies are defied by circumstance and brute political reality.

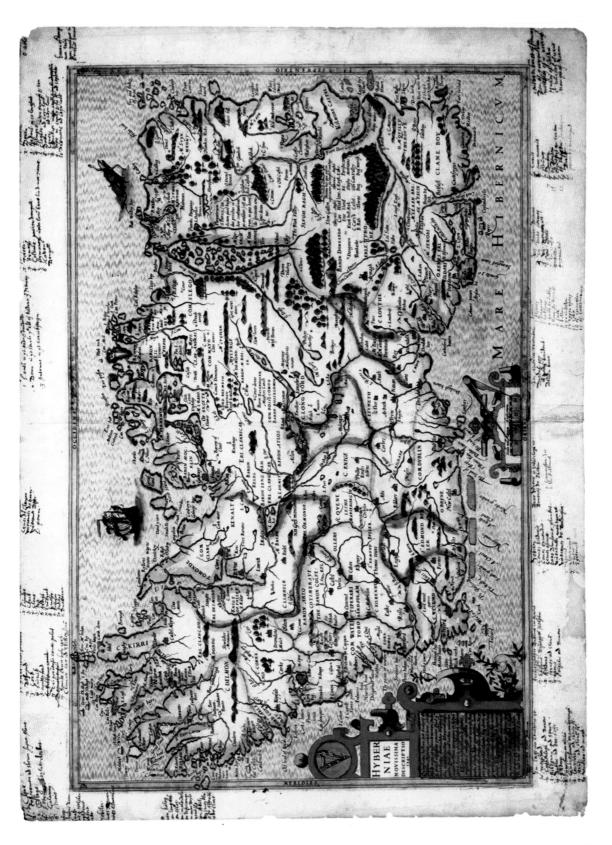

CHRONOLOGY

1558	Accession of Elizabeth I following the death of Mary I. The state-supported Reformation unpopular in Ireland.
1565–71	Sir Henry Sidney Governor of Ireland.
1569–71	Parliament declares the Lordship of Tyrone under the power of the Crown. Revolts in Munster, Leinster and Connacht against the policy.
1571–75	Sir William FitzWilliam Governor of Ireland.
1573	Private colonisation ventures continue in Ulster.
1576	Reappointed Sidney launches conciliatory policy halting any further private colonisation.
1579–80	Rebellion in Munster, exacerbated by a second revolt in Leinster led by James Eustace, Viscount Baltinglass and Feagh Mac Hugh O'Byrne. Support from discontented Palesmen. Arthur Lord Grey de Wilton is given the position of Governor to deal with the 'dual revolt'. Defeated at Glenmalure in Wicklow but successful at Smerwick.
1582–83	The suppression of both revolts in Munster and Leinster culminates in the killing of Earl of Desmond.
1595	Rebellion of Hugh O'Neill, Earl of Tyrone.
1598	O'Neill victorious at Yellow Ford, Ulster.
1601	O'Donnell, O'Neill and Spaniards defeated by Mountjoy at the Battle of Kinsale.
1603	The accession of James I leads to the enforcement of English law in Ireland, especially Ulster. Hugh O'Donnell and Earl of Tyrone surrender.
1607	The 'Flight of the Earls': O'Neill, Earl of Tyrone, O'Donnell, Earl of Tyrconnell.
1608	Plantation of Derry (City of London). Six other confiscated counties planned.
1641	Great Catholic-Gaelic rebellion for return of lands. Ireland thrown into chaos.
1642	Irish suppression hoped for by English Parliament with the 'Adventurers Act'. Robert Munro and army land in Ulster in April. Civil War in England. Catholic Confederation assembles at Kilkenny.
1649	Execution of Charles I. Cromwell's arrival in Ireland leads to capture of Drogheda, Wexford, New Ross. There follows a Cromwellian conquest and subsequent implementation of plantations.

1658	Death of Cromwell.
1660	Restoration period – accession of Charles II. Upholds Cromwellian conquest but restores property to 'innocent papists'.
1665	'Act of Explanation' obliges grantees of Cromwell to surrender one third of their lands to 'innocents'.
1685	Accession of James II.
1686–87	The newly appointed Earl of Tyrconnell, Richard Talbot, replaces Protestant officials with Catholics.
1688	Deposition of James II in England. Gates of Derry closed to James' troops.
1690	William of Orange defeats Jacobites at Boyne.
1695	Fourteen per cent of Irish land held by Catholics. Rights of Catholics restricted in education, arms-bearing and horse owning, and the Catholic clergy banished.
1699	Acts restricting Irish woollen exports.
1704	Catholics' presence restricted in landholding and public offices.
1713	Jonathan Swift becomes Dean of St Patrick's.
1728	Act removing franchise from Catholics.
1742	First performance of Handel's *Messiah* in Fishamble Street Music Hall.
1775	Henry Grattan leader of Patriot opposition in Irish Parliament.
1782	Irish Parliament successful in gaining 'legislative independence' from British.
1791	Wolfe Tone's *Argument on Behalf of the Catholics of Ireland*. Leads to foundation of Society of United Irishmen.
1792	Relief Act allows Catholics to practise law.
1796–98	United Irishmen plotting rebellion. Rebellion in Wexford in May 1798. Humbert lands in Killala in August. Tone arrested and dies in November.
1800	Act of Union – Ireland governed henceforth by Westminster.
1803	Robert Emmet's rising, trial and execution.
1822	Irish Constabulary Act (establishing county police forces and a salaried magistracy).
1823	Catholic Association founded, led by Daniel O'Connell.
1828	O'Connell elected for County Clare.
1829	Catholic Emancipation passed.
1837	Accession of Queen Victoria.
1840	O'Connell's Repeal Association founded.

1842	*The Nation* newspaper founded by Thomas Davis.
1843	O'Connell's 'Monster Meetings' for Repeal of the Union.
1845	Blight in the potato harvest. Beginning of Great Famine (1845–49).
1846	Repeal of Corn Laws. August sees Public Works started but stopped due to expectation of new harvest. Total failure of potato harvest. Public Works restarted. October sees first deaths from starvation.
1847	Foundation of Irish Confederation. Free rations first handed out from Government soup kitchens.
1848–49	Worst years of Great Famine. Rebellion by Young Ireland movement. Battle of the Widow McCormack's Cabbage Garden at Ballingarry.
1858	After James Stephens returns from France he establishes the Irish Republican Brotherhood. Fenian Brotherhood founded in the USA.
1861	Beginning of American Civil War.
1866	Archbishop Paul Cullen becomes the first Irish Cardinal.
1867	Attempted Fenian rising.
1869	Disestablishment of the Church of Ireland by W.E. Gladstone's government.
1870	Gladstone's first Land Act recognising tenant's right (August) and the foundation of Home Government Association by Isaac Butt (September).
1875	Charles Stewart Parnell elected MP for County Meath.
1879	Threat of famine in Ireland. Irish National Land League founded, instigated by Michael Davitt, widespread evictions.
1879–82	Land War.
1881	Gladstone's second Land Act.
1886	First Home Rule Bill.
1891	Parnell marries Katharine O'Shea (June), dies at Brighton (October).
1893	Second Home Rule Bill. Gaelic League founded.
1898	United Irish League founded.
1900	John Redmond elected chairman of Irish Parliamentary Party and United Irish League.
1907	Dockers' strike and riots in Belfast.
1914	Illegal importation of arms by Ulster Volunteers and Irish Volunteers. Buckingham Palace conference collapses just before outbreak of World War I.
1915	Reorganisation of the Irish Republican Brotherhood and formation of military council (December).

1916	Irish Republic proclaimed in Dublin (24 April). There follows martial law, rebel surrender, imprisonments and 16 executions. The Ulster Division also loses significant numbers in the Battle of the Somme.
1917	The Irish Convention ineffectual and Sinn Féin and Irish Volunteers reorganise.
1918	The General Election sees Republican success and the formation of Dáil Éireann in following January.
1920	The Government of Ireland Act introduces partition between two Home Rule states. Dublin's 'Bloody Sunday'.
1921	IRA setback. King opens Northern Ireland Parliament in Belfast. Sir James Craig Prime Minister in Northern Ireland. A truce is called. December witnesses Anglo-Irish Treaty.
1922	Convention of Anti-Treaty IRA. 'Special' powers given to Northern Ireland police. National Army given emergency powers after death of Collins. Irish Free State established.
1923	End of Civil War – IRA 'dump arms'. Free State admitted to League of Nations.
1924	National Army re-organisation, cutbacks and threatened mutiny.
1925	Partition confirmed by tripartite agreement.
1926	De Valera founds Fianna Fáil. General election in Free State.
1929	Proportional representation abolished in Northern Ireland.
1930	Irish Labour Party and TU Congress separate.
1931	Banning of the IRA in Free State.
1932	In the general election Fianna Fáil prove successful.
1933	National Guard (Blueshirts) formed. United Ireland Party (Fine Gael) formed under O'Duffy (Blueshirts leader).
1934	Cosgrave reinstated as O'Duffy resigns.
1935	Importation and sale of contraceptives banned in Free State.
1936	Free State Senate abolished.
1937	Constitution of Éire replaces Free State.
1938	UK agree to subsidise Northern Ireland Social Welfare payments to UK standards.
1939	IRA bombing campaign on Great Britain in World War II. Éire neutral.
1940	Death of IRA hunger strikers in Éire. Anglo-Irish military consultations. Economic sanctions imposed on Éire.
1941	The most destructive German air raids on Belfast and Dublin. Death of James Joyce.

1945	Congress of Irish Unions formed after split in Trade Union Congress. Churchill's and de Valera's radio speeches post-World War II.
1946	Northern Ireland National Insurance aligned with Great Britain.
1948	NHS introduced in Northern Ireland — Irish Republic enacted after Costello's repeal of External Relations Act. Fianna Fáil lose election, de Valera out of office after 16 years.
1949	Ireland Act, agreement that partition will be perpetuated.
1954	IRA attacks in Armagh.
1955	Republic admitted to UNO.
1956–62	Border campaign initiated by IRA.
1958	First programme for economic expansion in the Republic.
1961	Republic unsuccessful in joining EEC.
1964	Lemass-O'Neill talks held on reconciliation.
1966	Anglo-Irish Free Trade Agreement.
1967	NI Civil Rights Association founded.
1968	First Civil Rights march. Clash in Derry between CRA and police. O'Neill's programme for the removal of discrimination against Catholics in local government, housing and franchise.
1969	People's Democracy march from Belfast to Derry in January. There follows a series of explosions. Chichester Clark becomes Prime Minister. British troops sent in.
1970	Dublin Arms Trial. Splits in Sinn Féin and IRA lead to provisional factions setting up.
1971	Paisley's Democratic Unionist Party founded. Re-introduction of internment. First British soldier killed by IRA in Belfast.
1972	Following Derry's Bloody Sunday in January, direct rule is imposed.
1973	Republic, UK and NI join EEC. Proportional representation restored in NI (December). Sunningdale Agreement fails.
1974	Multiple deaths in Dublin bombing. Guildford and Birmingham pub bombings in November and December.
1975	NI internment suspended.
1976	British ambassador in Dublin killed. Republic's Emergency Powers Bill referred to Supreme Court by President.
1978	Twelve killed by Provisionals' fire bombs in a Co. Down restaurant.
1979	Earl Mountbatten and relations killed in Co. Sligo. Eighteen soldiers killed at Warrenpoint, Co. Down.
1979	Visit of Pope John Paul II.
1981	Deaths of Republican hunger-strikers.

1982	Killings of soldiers at Knightsbridge (July) and Ballykelly, Co. Derry, (December).
1983	Referendum bans abortion in Republic.
1985	Anglo-Irish Agreement signed at Hillsborough. Unionists bitterly opposed to its terms.
1986	Confirmation of Republic's ban on divorce.
1987	Eleven killed by IRA before Enniskillen service on Remembrance Sunday.
1989	Fianna Fáil form coalition government for the first time in their history following general election. Their partners are the Progressive Democrats. Charles Haughey remains Taoiseach.
1990	Republic of Ireland reach quarter-finals of the soccer world cup in Italy under the management of Jack Charlton.
1990	Mary Robinson elected seventh President of Ireland, the first woman to hold the office.
1992	Dr Eamon Casey, Bishop of Galway, flees country after it was revealed that he had fathered a child in the course of an affair nearly 20 years previously. The first of a succession of sexual scandals that eroded the authority of the Catholic Church in the course of the decade.
1994	IRA and Loyalist paramilitary groups announce ceasefire.
1996	In the Republic of Ireland, a constitutional referendum to permit civil divorce and re-marriage is carried narrowly.
1996	Canary Wharf bombing marks end of IRA ceasefire.
1997	Following Labour victory in British general election, Dr Marjorie (Mo) Mowlam appointed first woman Secretary of State for Northern Ireland.
1997	Fianna Fáil-PD coalition under Bertie Ahern replaces Rainbow coalition (Fine Gael, Labour, Democratic Left) following general election in the Republic.
1997	IRA declare a resumption of the 1994 ceasefire (July).
Autumn 1997–Spring 1998	Former US Senator, George Mitchell, chairs negotiations at Stormont.
10 April 1998	Good Friday Agreement signed by all parties except DUP.
2 May 1998	Agreement ratified by large majorities throughout Ireland.
15 August 1998	Omagh bombing kills 31 and dashes euphoria.
2 December 1999	After several failed attempts, new devolved power-sharing government meets for first time.
11 February 2000	Northern Executive suspended because of Unionist insistence on IRA decommissioning.
1 June 2000	Executive restored after IRA commitment 'to put arms beyond use'.

SELECT BIBLIOGRAPHY

Arthur, Paul; *The People's Democracy 1968–73*, Belfast 1974.

Bartlett, Thomas; *The Fall and Rise of the Irish Nation*, Dublin 1992.

Bartlett, Thomas & Hayton, David, eds; *Penal Era and Golden Age: essays in Irish history 1690–1800*, Belfast 1979.

Bew, Paul; *Land and the National Question, 1858–82*, Dublin 1979.

Bew, Paul & Gillespie, Gordon, eds; *Northern Ireland, A Chronology of the Troubles 1968–99*, Dublin 1999.

Bowman, John; *De Valera and the Ulster Question, 1917–73*, Oxford 1982.

Boyce, George; *Nineteenth-Century Ireland: the search for stability*, Dublin 1990.

Brooke, Peter; *Ulster Presbyterianism: the historical perspective 1610–1970*, Dublin 1987.

Bruce, Steve; *The Red Hand: Protestant paramilitaries in Ireland*, Oxford 1992.

Bull, Philip; *Land, Politics and Nationalism: a study of the Irish land question*, Dublin 1996.

Callanan, Frank; *The Parnell Split 1890–91*, Cork 1992.

Clarke, Samuel; *Social Origins of the Irish Land War*, Princeton, 1979.

Clarke, Samuel & Donnelly, Jr, James S., eds; *Irish Peasants, Violence and Political Unrest, 1780–1914*, Manchester, 1983.

Caulfield, Max; *The Easter Rebellion*, Dublin 1995.

Comerford, R.V.; *The Fenians in Context: Irish Politics and Society 1848–1882*, Dublin 1985.

Connolly, S.J.; *Priests and People in Pre-Famine Ireland 1780–1845*, Dublin 1982.

Connolly, S.J., ed.; *The Oxford Companion to Irish History*, Oxford 1998.

Coogan, Tim Pat; *The IRA*, London 1980.

Coogan, Tim Pat; *de Valera: Long Fellow, Long Shadow*, Dublin 1993.

Coogan, Tim Pat; *Michael Collins: A Biography*, London 1990.

Curran, Joseph M.; *The Birth of the Irish Free State, 1921–23*, Alabama 1980.

Davis, Richard; *The Young Ireland Movement*, Dublin 1987.

De Burca, Marcus; *The GAA: A History*, Dublin 1999.

Dickson, David; *Old World Colony: Cork and South Munster 1630–1830*, Cork 2005.

Dudley Edwards, Ruth; *Patrick Pearse: The Triumph of Failure*, London 1977.

Elliott, Marianne; *Wolfe Tone: Prophet of Irish Independence*, New Haven 1989.

Elliott, Marianne; *The Catholics of Ulster: a history*, London 2000.

Elliott, Sidney & Flax, W.D.; *Northern Ireland: A Political Directory*, Belfast 1989.

Ferriter, Diarmaid; *The Transformation of Ireland 1900–2000*, London 2004.

Fisk, Robert; *In Time of War: Ireland, Ulster and the Price of Neutrality, 1939–45*, London 1983.

Fitzpatrick, David; *Politics and Irish Life 1913–21: Provincial Experiences of War and Revolution*, Dublin 1977.

Foster, R.F.; *Modern Ireland 1660–1972*, London 1988.

Garvin, Tom; *The Evolution of Irish Nationalist Politics*, Dublin 1981.

Garvin, Tom; *Nationalist Revolutionaries in Ireland*, Dublin 1987.

Garvin, Tom; *1922: The Birth of Irish Democracy*, Dublin 1996.

Garvin, Tom; *Preventing the Future*, Dublin 2004.

Girvin, Brian; *Between Two Worlds: Politics and*

Economy in Independent Ireland, Dublin 1989.

Girvin, Brian; *The Emergency: Neutral Ireland 1939–1945*, London 2006.

Hart, Peter; *The IRA and its Enemies: Violence and Community in County Cork 1916–1923*, Oxford 1998.

Hickey, D.J. & Doherty, J.E., eds.; *A New Dictionary of Irish History from 1800*, Dublin 2003.

Hopkinson, Michael; *Green Against Green: The Irish Civil War*, Dublin 1998.

Hopkinson, Michael; *The Irish War of Independence*, Dublin 2002.

Hoppen, K. Theodore; *Elections, Politics and Society in Ireland, 1832–1885*, Oxford 1984.

Horgan, John; *Sean Lemass: The Enigmatic Patriot*, Dublin 1997.

Jackson, Alvin; *Ireland 1798–1988*, Oxford 1999.

Keogh, Daire; *The French Disease: the Catholic Church and Radicalism in Ireland 1790–1800*, Dublin 1993.

Keogh, Dermot; *Ireland and Europe 1919–89*, Cork 1989.

Keogh, Dermot; *Twentieth-Century Ireland: Revolution and State Building*, Dublin 2005.

Kinealy, Christine; *This Great Calamity: The Irish Famine 1845–52*, Dublin 1994.

Lalor, Brian, ed.; *The Encyclopaedia of Ireland*, Dublin 2003.

Lyons, F.S.L.; *Charles Stewart Parnell*, London 1977.

Lyons, F.S.L.; *Culture and Anarchy in Ireland, 1890–1939*, Oxford 1979.

MacDonagh, Oliver; *O'Connell: The Life of Daniel O'Connell, 1775–1847*, London 1991.

McGee, Owen; *The Irish Republican Brotherhood from the Land League to Sinn Féin*, Dublin 2005.

Maume, Patrick; *D.P. Moran*, Dublin 1995.

Miller, David W.; *Church, Station and Nation in Ireland, 1898–1921*, Dublin 1973.

Miller, David W.; *Queen's Rebels: Ulster Loyalism in Historical Perspective*, Dublin 1978.

Mitchell, Arthur; *Revolutionary Government in Ireland: Dáil Éireann, 1919–22*, Dublin 1995.

Mokyr, Joel; *Why Ireland Starved*, London 1985.

Moody, T.W., ed.; *The Fenian Movement*, Cork 1968.

Moody, T.W.; *Davitt and Irish Revolution, 1846–82*, Oxford 1981.

O'Brien, Conor Cruise; *States of Ireland*, London 1972.

O'Day, Alan; *Irish Home Rule, 1867–1921*, Manchester 1988.

O'Ferrall, Fergus; *Catholic Emancipation: Daniel O'Connell and the Birth of Irish Democracy 1820–30*, Dublin 1985.

Ó Gráda, Cormac; *Ireland and New Economic History 1780–1939*, Oxford 1994.

O'Halpin, Eunan; *The Decline of the Union: British Government in Ireland, 1892–1920*, Dublin 1987.

Rumpf, Erhard & Hepburn, A.C.; *Nationalism and Socialism in Twentieth-Century Ireland*, Liverpool, 1977.

Stewart, A.T.Q.; *The Ulster Crisis: Resistance to Home Rule, 1912–14*, London 1967.

Stewart, A.T.Q.; *The Narrow Ground: Aspects of Ulster, 1609–1969*, London 1977.

Taylor, Peter; *Provos: The IRA and Sinn Féin*, London 1997.

Townshend, Charles; *Political Violence in Ireland: Government and Resistance since 1848*, Oxford 1983

Townshend, Charles; *Easter 1916: The Irish Rebellion*, London 2003.

Whelan, Kevin; *The Tree of Liberty: Radicalism, Catholicism and the Construction of Irish Identity, 1760–1830*, Cork 1996.

Whyte, J.H.; *Church and State in Modern Ireland, 1923–1979*, Dublin 1980.

Wright, Frank; *Northern Ireland: A Comparative Analysis*, Dublin 1988.

INDEX

References in this index in **bold** face are maps or graphs and in *italic* face are illustrations.

ACKNOWLEDGEMENTS

The publishers would like to thank the following:

Alamy Images   46, 94
Camera Press Ireland   149
Corbis/Yann Arthus-Bertrand   125
Courtesy of the ESB   152
Defence Force Headquarters   179
Getty Images/AFP   194
Getty Images/Hulton Archive   91, 112, 106, 135, 154, 166
Getty Images/Time Life Pictures   117, 165
Hulton Picture Library   102
Illustrated London News   23, 45, 56, 67, 73, 74
Irish Image Collection   81, 138
Inpho   126
National Gallery of Ireland   17, 19, 32, 114
National Library of Ireland   52, 61, 62, 96, 144B
Pacemaker Press International   184
Peter Newark Historical Pictures   11, 12, 13, 52
Photocall Ireland   175, 196
Private Collection   20, 24, 94, 106, 119, 120, 138, 146, 148
R.L.P.P.M&A. Ltd   28, 209
RTE Stills Library   147, 176
Ryanair   194
St Patrick's College, Drumcondra   76
Topfoto   173, 181, 182
Trustees of the National Museums of Northern Ireland   98

Cartography and Design: Jeanne Radford, Malcolm Swanston and Jonathan Young